Index of Watchtower Errors

1879 to 1989

David A. Reed, Editor

Compiled by
Steve Huntoon and
John Cornell

BAKER BOOK HOUSE
Grand Rapids, Michigan 49516

Copyright © 1990 by Baker Books
a division of Baker Book House Company
P.O. Box 6287, Grand Rapids, MI 49516-6287

ISBN: 0-8010-7756-7

Fourth printing, December 1994

Printed in the United States of America

Contents

4

About the Editor

David A. Reed became a baptized Jehovah's Witness in 1969. He served the Watch Tower Society as a full-time minister, an elder, and a presiding overseer. Eventually, personal Bible reading caused him to question the organization's teachings, and this led to his formal expulsion in 1982.

After embracing biblical Christianity he began writing articles and tracts with the aim of evangelizing Jehovah's Witnesses. Today he is the publisher and editor of *Comments from the Friends,* a quarterly on the JWs; president of Gospel Truth Ministries, Inc.; editor of *The Gospel Truth,* which deals with cults in general; and a contributing editor of *Christian Research Journal,* a publication of Christian Research Institute. His other books include:

Behind the Watchtower Curtain
Jehovah's Witnesses Answered Verse by Verse
How to Rescue Your Loved One from the Watchtower

Preface

Credit for this volume belongs to Steve Huntoon and John Cornell. They originally compiled lists of Watch Tower quotes on their personal computers for their own use in refuting error. (John formerly operated the New York branch of Alpha and Omega Ministries, and Steve ministers informally by distributing enlightening cassette tapes on cult-related topics.) Steve sent me a printout of his list to help me in researching articles for my quarterly newsletter *Comments from the Friends,* which focuses on Jehovah's Witnesses.

The chronological listing Steve sent me was impressive, and I immediately informed him of my desire to make it available to others by publishing it through my ministry. Then, having secured his approval, I set about the laborious task of typesetting it. In the meantime, Steve had informed John Cornell of my project, and John sent me a printout of his list of similar quotes arranged according to subject. The two lists complemented each other and served as a fairly complete catalogue of quotes useful in refuting Jehovah's Witnesses.

The more time I spent typesetting, combining, adding to, refining, and editing the two lists, the more convinced I became that this information should be made available to the entire Christian community. With over nine million people attending Jehovah's Witness Kingdom Halls worldwide, and nearly half of these devotees actively distributing Watchtower literature from house to house, Christians should have access to a catalogue of the errors this literature contains. I take this opportunity to thank Baker Book House for sharing that conviction and choosing to publish this *Index.*

Introduction

To Jehovah's Witnesses, the Watch Tower Bible and Tract Society is God's sole channel for communicating *truth* to humankind today. Persons associated with the Watch Tower Society are considered to be "in the truth"—as opposed to outsiders who are "of the world." Just as Christians speak of being "in the Lord" by virtue of having accepted Jesus Christ as their personal Savior and Lord, in like manner Jehovah's Witnesses speak of being "in the truth" by virtue of having accepted the Watch Tower Society as God's "channel of communication."

So, the very mention of *error* in connection with the Watch Tower is enough to throw JWs into mental turmoil. How can the organization they call "the truth" be guilty of error? How can it be so full of errors that an *Index* listing the Watch Tower's major mistakes, doctrinal changes, false prophecies, frauds, and deceptions fills an entire volume? Hopefully this *Index* will prove such a challenge to the Jehovah's Witnesses who come across it that they will actually use it to verify the Watch Tower quotes and references listed.

Although most outsiders are unaware of such a restriction, Jehovah's Witnesses know well that they are forbidden to read the literature of other religious organizations. They have been told that "it would be foolhardy, as well as a waste of valuable time, for Jehovah's Witnesses to accept and expose themselves to false religious literature that is designed to deceive" (WT, 5/1/1984, p. 31). And they have been taught that "reading apostate publications" is "similar to reading pornographic literature" (WT, 3/15/1986, p. 14). Any who violate these commandments by reading non-JW religious material face trial before a closed-door "judicial committee" with the possibility of being "disfellowshiped"—expelled from the congregation and shunned by all former associates, even family.

For this reason books refuting Watch Tower teachings are seldom read by Jehovah's Witnesses. Only one who is already considering leaving the sect will accept the risks involved. Even then, precautions are taken. I have received letters from Witnesses who pulled such a forbidden book off the shelf at a bookstore or library, quickly read portions of it (all the while glancing furtively about lest they be observed and reported to the elders), and then replaced the book and slipped out of the building, only to return after a few days for another clandestine encounter. One JW told me how, after anonymously purchasing such a book, he ripped off the cover and threw it away, keeping only the pages so that anyone who spotted him reading it could not easily identify what it was.

But the Witnesses who look up the materials cited in this *Index* need not worry about being caught reading forbidden books written by "apostate" ex-JWs. Rather, they will be looking deeply into the publications of their own organization. And, instead of venturing onto the foreign turf of a Christian bookstore or public library, they will be pulling books off the familiar shelves of the "Theocratic Library" in their own Kingdom Hall. So they should have no reason to fear, *if* they are really "in the *truth*."

What if the Watch Tower publications cited reveal that the organization is a false prophet—not simply having made an occasional mistake, but having promulgated false prophecies repeatedly throughout its history? What if the prophetic dates were presented by the leaders as "God's dates, not ours" as stated by the *Watch Tower* of July 15, 1894 (Reprints, p. 1677)? Then the sincere Witness must pay special attention to God's words at Deuteronomy 18:20–22 (Watch Tower's *New World Translation*):

> . . . the prophet who presumes to speak in my name a word that I have not commanded him to speak . . . that prophet must die. And in case you should say in your heart: "How shall we know the word that Jehovah has not spoken?" when the prophet speaks in the name of Jehovah and the word does not occur or come true, that is the word that Jehovah did not speak. With presumptuousness the prophet spoke it.

Jesus foretold that "false prophets will arise and will give great signs and wonders to mislead, if possible, even the cho-

10

sen ones. Look! I have forewarned you" (Matt. 24:24, 25 N.W.T.). A Witness confronted with the evidence must choose between obeying Christ or continuing to follow the Watchtower Society.

And the evidence is overwhelming! Referenced in this *Index* are over one hundred false prophetic declarations the organization has published as "the truth," besides more than six hundred other statements equally damaging to the leadership's credibility. Taken together, these over seven hundred pieces of evidence demand a verdict of "guilty on all counts." The Jehovah's Witnesses who examine these references will be forced to admit that the organization they have been following is not what it claims to be.

This *Index* should be an effective tool in the hands of Christians reaching out to Jehovah's Witnesses. When Christians attempt to share the gospel with them using the Bible alone, Witnesses simply respond with their own favorite proof texts, and the discussion degenerates into a Scripture-trading match. The problem is that Witnesses do not really look to the Bible as the final authority on what to believe. They have been convinced that their leaders represent God's "channel of communication" and that, "unless we are in touch with this channel of communication that God is using, we will not progress along the road to life, no matter how much Bible reading we do" (WT, 12/1/1981, p. 27). Since it is their organization's interpretation of what the Bible says that determines JWs' beliefs, those beliefs cannot be challenged effectively without first undermining the authority of the organization. And that is what is accomplished by the use of damaging quotations from the Society's publications. Its claim to being God's "channel of communication" falls into question when it communicates many ideas that could not possibly have come from God, including false prophecies as mentioned above.

In addition to false prophecies, the sect's books and magazines contain a permanent record of many peculiar teachings, doctrinal vacillations, and deadly errors taught over the years as "the truth." From the beginning until 1953, for example, Almighty God was said not to be omnipresent but rather to reside upon the star Alcyone in the Pleiades star system (see "Pleiades," p. 95). The inhabitants of the ancient city of Sodom were dragged in and out of the grave as the organization kept changing its teaching on whether or not they would be resurrected. The answer was Yes in 1879, No in 1952, Yes in 1965, and No in 1988 (see "Resurrection of Sodomites," p. 116). And, crossing from the academic to the real world, between the years 1931 and 1952 vaccinations were prohibited, and during the years 1967 to 1980 organ transplants were banned. Those medical procedures are now permitted again, but who knows how many Witnesses or their children got sick or died during the interim for lack of a vaccination or for want of a kidney or cornea transplant? (A former JW elder in England told reporters that he resigned after a woman in his congregation turned down a cornea transplant in obedience to the Watch Tower and went blind.) How high will the death toll climb—already estimated by some to be in the thousands—as loyal followers continue to refuse blood transfusions, adhering to an interpretation introduced in the 1940s but not yet rescinded (see "Blood, Vaccination, Transplants," p. 68)?

Rather than discuss other strange teachings here, we leave it to the reader to examine the evidence on the pages that follow. As its documented errors pile up, the organization's claim to being "the truth" erodes. Remember, the testimony presented in this volume is not that of the Watch Tower's critics, enemies, or accusers; on the contrary, it consists of statements by leaders and spokesmen writing in their official capacity in the organization's books and magazines. As Jesus said, "by your words you will be condemned" (Matt. 12:37).

How to Use the Index

Chronological Listing

This section features statements from the Watchtower Society's magazines arranged in the order in which they appeared from 1879 to 1989. This material can be scanned to identify teachings or prophecies unique to any given time period, or the entire section can be read to reveal how teachings changed over the years.

Subject Listing

The subjects are grouped alphabetically, and the statements under each subject are listed chronologically (with the exception that doctrinal changes may be placed next to each other for contrast).

Some statements are quoted, while others are paraphrased or condensed for the sake of space and ease of identification. For the key to abbreviated titles see Appendix 4.

Some true statements are included in the listings if Watch Tower publications elsewhere contradict or reverse themselves on these points. For example, "Christ to Be Worshiped," p. 127 (Make Sure '53, p. 85) is listed because a later publication states: "No distinct worship is to be rendered to Jesus Christ" (WT, 1/1/1954, p. 31). Statements of unorthodox doctrine that have been repeated countless times over the years are not normally listed unless contradicted elsewhere. In each case, usefulness in argumentation has been the chief factor in determining selections.

Additional Features
1. Abbreviated titles are expanded in the bibliography.
2. Magazine page numbers refer to bound volume reprints.
3. Photo-documentation sources are listed in Appendix 3.

Please send corrections or suggested additions to:
David A. Reed, P. O. Box 840, Stoughton, MA 02072.

Chronological Listing

The men of Sodom will be resurrected.

WT 7/1879, p. 8

"A *truth* presented by Satan himself is just *as true* as a *truth* stated by God. . . . Accept truth wherever you find it, no matter what it contradicts."

WT 7/1879, pp. 8–9

"'Let all the angels of God worship him' [that must include Michael, the chief angel, hence Michael is not the Son of God]."

WT 11/1879, p. 48

"to worship Christ in any form cannot be wrong"

WT 3/1880, p. 83

". . . the '*New* Covenant' is a thing of the future."

WT 6/1880, p. 110

New light never contradicts old light, but adds to it.

WT 2/1881, p. 188

"The 'grand gallery' measures 1874 inches long at the top, 1878 inches long at a groove cut in its sides about midway between bottom and top and 1881 inches, at the bottom. . . . Now notice how aptly these three distinct dates (1874, 1878, 1881,) are marked by the pyramid. . . ."

WT 5/1881, p. 225

chronological diagram featuring pyramids

WT 9/1881, p. 272

Direct quotes are in quotation marks; other material is paraphrased or condensed.

15

"Blessed is that Servant (the whole body of Christ)"
WT 11/1881, p. 291

". . . the same titles are applicable to the Church as his body. . . . soon follows the power which will, under him as our head, constitute the whole body of Christ the 'Mighty God' . . . the members of that company which as a whole will be the *Everlasting Father. . . .*"
WT 11/1881, p. 298

"Now we appear like men, and all die naturally like men, but in the resurrection we will rise in our true character as Gods."
WT 12/1881, p. 301

"Three Gods in one person, or as some put it, one God in three persons."
WT 7/1882, p. 369

"We believe that a visible organization, and the adoption of some particular name, would tend to increase our numbers and make us more respectable in the estimation of the world. . . . But . . . We always refuse to be called by any other name than that of our Head—Christians. . . ."
WT 3/1883, p. 458

". . . the New Covenant is now in force, having been sealed by the blood, the death of Christ."
WT 9/1887, p. 974

We are convinced that the *Watch Tower* is God's chosen vessel for dispensing "meat in due season."
WT 1/1890, p. 1171

". . . the Scriptural declaration that the Millennium of peace and blessing would be introduced by forty years of trouble, beginning slightly in 1874 and increasing until social chaos should prevail in 1914."
WT 10/1890, p. 1243

cross and crown symbol
WT 1/1/1891, p. 1277

"The date of the close of that 'battle' is definitely marked in Scripture as October, 1914. It is already in progress, its beginning dating from October, 1874."
WT 1/15/1892, p. 1355

"And although we are nowhere instructed to make petitions to him, it evidently could not be improper to do so; for such a course is nowhere prohibited, and the disciples worshiped him."

WT 5/15/1892, p. 1410

Jesus is called the Almighty at Revelation 1:8.

WT 4/15/1893, p. 1515

"The endeavor to compel all men to think alike on all subjects, culminated in the great apostasy and the development of the great Papal system. . . ."

WT 9/1/1893, p. 1572

There is no organization today clothed with authority.

WT 9/1/1893, p. 1573

If you get a tract or paper from us that is not in harmony with the Scriptures, let us know and do not circulate it.

WT 3/1/1894, p. 1629

There is no reason for changing the figures; they are God's dates, not ours; 1914 is not the date for the beginning, but the end!

WT 7/15/1894, p. 1677

The end of 6000 years is 1873.

WT 7/15/1894, p. 1675

A visible organization is out of harmony with God's divine plan.

WT 12/1/1894, p. 1743

". . . those who believe in him . . . 'Blessed is that *servant.*' . . . they must be wise and faithful servants. . . ."

WT 4/1/1895, p. 1797

". . . the group Pleiades. And the reasonable suggestion has been made that that center may be the heaven of heavens, the highest heaven, the throne of God."

WT 5/15/1895, p. 1814

"Beware of 'organization.' It is wholly unnecessary."

WT 9/15/1895, p. 1866

God's plan for the ages is in the Millennial Dawn; it is God's mouthpiece.

WT 9/15/1895, p. 1867

In our issue of April 1, 1895, we applied "that servant" to *all* servants of God, but further examination points to *one* individual servant.

WT 3/1/1896, p. 47

"The most reasonable suggestion we know of . . . namely, that heaven is located in or in connection with the heavenly group, *Pleiades.*"

WT 12/1/1896, p. 2075

"If, therefore, we were drafted, and if the government refused to accept our conscientious scruples against warfare . . . we should request to be assigned . . . to some other non-combatant place of usefulness. . . . If not, and we ever got into battle, we might help to terrify the enemy, but need not shoot anybody."

WT 7/1/1898, p. 2332

"Yes, we believe our Lord Jesus while on earth was really worshipped, and properly so. While he was not *the* God, Jehovah, he was *a* God."

WT 7/15/1898, p. 2337

"no command in the Scriptures against military service"

WT 8/1/1898, p. 2345

" . . . the common thought of Trinitarians, that the Son *is* the Father."

WT 2/1/1899, p. 2434

Rev. William Draper, once black, is now white in answer to prayer.

WT 10/1/1900, p. 2706

The trouble in October 1914 is clearly marked in Scriptures; the severe trouble to start no later than 1910, with severe spasms between now and then.

WT 9/15/1901, p. 2876

"true that the white race exhibits some qualities of superiority over any other"

WT 7/15/1902, p. 3043

White people living in China eventually produce Chinese offspring—without intermarrying—due to the influence of soil and climate.

WT 7/15/1902, p. 3043

"nothing against our consciences in going into the army"
WT 4/15/1903, p. 3180

Romans 10:14 refers to Jesus.
WT 12/1/1903, p. 3282

It is quite immaterial the day Christmas is celebrated; we may properly join.
WT 12/15/1903, p. 3290

The "faithful and wise steward" would not be a company of individuals.
WT 4/15/1904, p. 3356

Don't quibble about the date; join in with the world and celebrate Christmas.
WT 12/1/1904, p. 3468

The Lord has a particular messenger commissioned as his representative.
WT 6/1/1905, p. 3570

Chronological chart; 1914 begins millennial age.
WT 6/15/1905, p. 3576

Mrs. Russell's view of who is the "faithful and wise servant"; one particular servant; "that servant"
WT 7/15/1906, p. 3811

"the truths I present as God's mouthpiece"
WT 7/15/1906, p. 3821

The *Studies in the Scriptures* suggested as Christmas gifts
WT 11/15/1907, p. 4094

". . . the work of the Christ in the inauguration of the New Covenant could not begin until the perfecting of his own body, which is the church. . . . and all of his blood has not yet been shed."
WT 4/1/1909, p. 4367

Abstaining from blood (Acts 15:29) "should be observed by all spiritual Israelites as representing the divine will."
WT 4/15/1909, p. 4374

"Bible classes and Bible studies all to no purpose until the Lord, in due time, sent them the 'Bible keys,' through the Society"
WT 10/1/1909, p. 4482

A person would go into darkness after two years of reading the Bible alone; would be in the light reading the *Studies in the Scriptures* alone.

WT 9/15/1910, p. 4685

"If the six volumes of SCRIPTURE STUDIES are practically the Bible topically arranged, with Bible proof-texts given, we might not improperly name the volumes—the Bible in an arranged form. That is to say, they are not merely comments on the Bible, but they are practically the Bible itself. . . ."

WT 9/15/1910, p. 4685

There has been no clear understanding of the Bible for centuries.

WT 9/15/1911, p. 4885

"Rather we should seek for dependent Bible study, rather than for independent Bible study."

WT 9/15/1911, p. 4885

"Any class leader who would make objection to a reference being made to *The Watch Tower* or to *Studies in the Scriptures* in connection with the discussion of any topic should properly be viewed with suspicion as a teacher."

WT 9/15/1911, p. 4885

"As already pointed out, we are by no means confident that this year, 1914, will witness as radical and swift changes of dispensation as we have expected."

WT 1/1/1914, p. 5373

"Armageddon may begin next spring, yet it is purely speculation to attempt to say just when."

WT 9/1/1914, p. 5527

"We did not say positively that this would be the year."

WT 11/1/1914, p. 5565

"The Battle of Armageddon, to which this war is leading . . . will signify the complete and everlasting overthrow of the wrong, and the permanent establishment of Messiah's righteous kingdom."

WT 4/1/1915, p. 5659

". . . the Pleiades may represent the residence of Jehovah, the place from which he governs the universe."

WT 6/15/1915, p. 5710

"Beloved brother . . . send you some slight token of the great love we have for you, as God's appointed servant and channel for dispensing the 'meat in due season' to the household of faith."

WT 11/15/1915, p. 5804

". . . our eyes of understanding should discern clearly the Battle of the Great Day of God Almighty now in progress. . . ."

WT 9/1/1916, p. 5951

At least three in the editorial committee have approved as truth every article in *The Watch Tower.*

WT 12/1/1916, p. 5997

A biography of Russell

WT 12/1/1916, p. 5997

Pastor Russell held closely to the Scriptures. He believed that Christ had been present since 1874. He also admitted in private to being that "Faithful and Wise Servant."

WT 12/1/1916, p. 5998

"Russell, thou hast, by the Lord been crowned a king . . . and thy enemies shall come and worship at thy feet."

WT 12/1/1916, p. 6015

The banner of Christ's presence on the title page of the *Watch Tower* will never come down until the Kingdom is known in all the earth.

WT 12/1/1916, p. 6015

To disregard the message received through Pastor Russell would mean disregard for the Lord.

WT 12/15/1916, p. 6024

Brother Rutherford said: "The Watch Tower Bible and Tract Society is the greatest corporation in the world, because from the time of its organization until now the Lord has used it as His channel through which to make known the glad tidings. . . ."

WT 1/15/1917, p. 6033

"Following the election Brother Rutherford, addressing the meeting, said . . . 'The policies which Brother Russell inaugurated I will attempt to carry forward.'"

WT 1/15/1917, pp. 6033–34

21

"*The Watch Tower* unhesitatingly proclaims brother Russell as 'that faithful and wise servant.'"

WT 3/1/1917, p. 6049

". . . every one in America should take pleasure in displaying the American flag."

WT 5/15/1917, p. 6086

"Since the Bethel Home was established, in one end of the Drawing Room there has been kept a small bust of Abraham Lincoln with two American flags displayed about the bust. This is deemed entirely proper. . . ."

WT 5/15/1917, p. 6086

"Truly there lived among us in these last days a prophet of the Lord. . . . his works remain an enduring witness to his wisdom and faithfulness!"

WT 6/1/1917, p. 6091

". . . the Great Pyramid, the measurements of which confirm the Bible teaching that 1878 marked the beginning of the harvest of the Gospel age. . . . the harvest would close forty years thereafter; to wit, in the spring of A.D. 1918. . . . we have only a few months in which to labor before the great night settles down when no man can work."

WT 10/1/1917, p. 6149

"There will be no slip-up. . . . Abraham should enter upon the actual possession of his promised inheritance in the year 1925 A.D."

WT 10/15/1917, p. 6157

The Scriptures indicate that Russell was chosen of the Lord from his birth. The two most popular messengers were Paul and Pastor Russell. Russell is the "servant" of Matthew 24:45–47.

WT 11/1/1917, p. 6159

"Hence our dear Pastor, now in glory, is without doubt, manifesting a keen interest in the harvest work, and is permitted by the Lord to exercise some strong influence thereupon."

WT 11/1/1917, p. 6161

The Finished Mystery was prepared under the direction of the Watchtower Bible and Tract Society.

WT 12/15/1917, p. 6182

22

"What will the year 1918 bring forth? . . . The Christian looks for the year to bring the full consummation of the church's hopes."

WT 1/1/1918, p. 6191

". . . we believe it is a safe rule to follow Brother Russell's interpretation, for the reason that he is the servant of the church, so constituted by the Lord for the Laodicean period; and therefore we should expect the Lord to teach us through him."

WT 2/15/1918, p. 6212

"That the harvest began in 1878, there is ample and convincing proof. The end of the harvest is due in the spring of 1918."

WT 5/1/1918, p. 6243

A narrow-minded Christian during wartime might object to serving with the Red Cross or buying government bonds, but a scripturally informed Christian sees it is proper to do both.

WT 6/1/1918, p. 6268

"Even treating the brother for a time as 'a heathen man and a publican' would not mean to do him injury, to castigate him, pillory him, or expose him to shame or contempt. . . . the brother may merely be treated in the kindly, courteous way in which it would be proper for us to treat any publican or Gentile. . . ."

WT 3/1/1919, p. 6397

"Is not the Watch Tower Bible and Tract Society the one and only channel which the Lord has used in dispensing his truth continually since the beginning of the harvest period?"

WT 4/1/1919, p. 6414

"our Lord himself has served us with the truth of Ezekiel and Revelation" (*The Finished Mystery*)

WT 4/1/1919, p. 6414

"No one in present truth for a moment doubts that brother Russell filled the office of the 'Faithful and Wise Servant.'"

WT 4/1/1920, p. 100

"We would not refuse to treat one as a brother because he did not believe the Society is the Lord's channel."

WT 4/1/1920, p. 100

23

"The Society by overwhelming majority vote expressed its will in substance thus: Brother Russell filled the office of 'that Servant.'"

WT 4/1/1920, p. 101

"That it [The Finished Mystery] contains some mistakes is freely admitted. Even the Bible contains some."

WT 4/1/1920, p. 103

It is the message of the hour, that must go to all Christendom: "Millions now living will never die."

WT 10/15/1920, p. 310

"Suppose you should be here in 1925, what would you do? I said I believe I will be home in the Pleiades before then."

WT 11/1/1920, p. 334

"The truth comes from the storehouse as the Lord sees necessary. . . . The Lord will open up truths as they are needed by the household of faith."

WT 6/15/1921, p. 182

Fulfilled prophecy—or physical facts—and the circumstantial evidence are conclusive proof that Russell filled the office of that faithful and wise servant.

WT 3/1/1922, p. 74

The Lord foretold an office that would be filled by man. The man the Lord chose to fill that office was his modest, humble, and faithful servant, brother Russell.

WT 5/1/1922, p. 135

Those in the truth got there by the ministry of Russell. To repudiate his work is equivalent to a repudiation of the Lord.

WT 5/1/1922, p. 132

In 1878 the process of setting up the kingdom began. The Lord raised the sleeping saints.

WT 6/1/1922, p. 174

"In the passages of the Great Pyramid of Gizeh the agreement of one or two measurements with present-truth chronology might be accidental, but the correspondency of dozens of measurements proves that the same God designed both pyramid and plan. . . ."

WT 6/15/1922, p. 187

24

"This chronology is not of man but of God . . . of divine origin . . . absolutely and unqualifiedly correct."

WT 7/15/1922, p. 217

"1914 ended the Gentile Times. . . . The date 1925 is even more distinctly indicated by the Scriptures. . . . by then the great crisis will be reached and probably passed."

WT 9/1/1922, p. 262

"No one can properly understand the work of God at this present time who does not realize that since 1874, the time of the Lord's return in power, there has been a complete change in God's operations."

WT 9/15/1922, p. 278

The loyalty test: God gave C. T. Russell to the church as a mouthpiece for him. Those who claim to have learned the truth apart from C. T. Russell are deceivers. Satan will cause people to think Russell was not the channel.

WT 9/15/1922, p. 279

Russell held the position of a steward; we hold this as a fact and a necessity of faith.

WT 12/15/1922, p. 396

"The Lord indicated he would use one member of his Church as the channel. . . ."

WT 3/1/1923, p. 68

"The Scriptures show that the second presence [of the Lord] was due in 1874. . . . This proof shows that the Lord has been present since 1874."

WT 3/1/1923, p. 67

When asked who the faithful and wise servant was, Russell would reply, "Some say I am while others say the Society is"; both are true, since Russell was in fact the Society.

WT 3/1/1923, p. 68

"1925 is definitely settled by the Scriptures. . . . the Christian has much more upon which to base his faith than Noah had (so far as the Scriptures reveal) upon which to base his faith in a coming deluge."

WT 4/1/1923, p. 106

"Charles Russell as the Laodicean messenger of the Church, faithfully filled the office of 'that Faithful and Wise Servant' while here on earth."

WT 12/1/1923, p. 360

"publish a volume setting forth the incidents of his [Russell's] life and work aside from and in addition to his personal writings"

WT 12/1/1923, p. 360

"Surely there is not the slightest room for doubt in the mind of a truly consecrated child of God that the Lord Jesus is present and has been since 1874."

WT 1/1/1924, p. 5

"The year 1925 is a date definitely and clearly marked in the Scriptures, even more clearly than that of 1914."

WT 7/15/1924, p. 211

"The year 1925 is here. With great expectation Christians have looked forward to this year. Many have confidently expected that all members of the body of Christ will be changed to heavenly glory during the year. This may be accomplished. It may not be."

WT 1/1/1925, p. 3

"The great Pyramid of Egypt, standing as a silent and inanimate witness of the Lord, is a messenger; and its testimony speaks with great eloquence concerning the divine plan."

WT 5/15/1925, p. 148

"It is to be expected that Satan will try to inject into the minds of the consecrated the thought that 1925 should see an end of the work, and that therefore it would be needless for them to do more."

WT 9/1/1925, p. 262

Some anticipated the work would end in 1925. The Lord did not so state.

WT 8/1/1926, p. 232

"The literature of the Society once plainly set forth that 1914 would mark the complete glorification of the Church."

WT 10/1/1926, p. 294

Christmas is so important, regardless of the date.

WT 12/15/1926, p. 371

"No truly great men have ever lived on earth since Jesus' time."

WT 1/1/1927, p. 7

"That Faithful and Wise Servant" does not apply to one individual and not to Brother Russell. Russell never made that claim himself.

WT 2/15/1927, p. 56

Sell as new truth, *Studies in the Scriptures.*

WT 3/15/1928, p. 126

"Sometimes a member of a class will refuse to engage in the canvasing for the books because there are some mistakes in the books. . . . As everyone knows, there are mistakes in the Bible. . . ."

WT 4/15/1928, p. 126

Everyone in present truth got their knowledge from the *Studies in the Scriptures.*

WT 4/15/1928, p. 126

"If the pyramid is not mentioned in the Bible, then following its teachings is being led by vain philosophy and false science and not following after Christ."

WT 11/15/1928, p. 341

"It is more reasonable to conclude that the great pyramid of Gizeh, as well as the other pyramids . . . were built . . . under the direction of Satan the Devil."

WT 11/15/1928, p. 344

"Then Satan put his knowledge into dead stone, which may be called Satan's Bible, and not God's stone witness. . . ."

WT 11/15/1928, p. 344

"Those who have devoted themselves to the pyramid . . . The mind of such was turned away from Jehovah and his Word."

WT 11/15/1928, p. 344

The Gospel of the Kingdom ceased to be proclaimed shortly after the death of the apostles. It was not preached again until after 1918.

WT 12/1/1928, pp. 363–64

Studies in the Scriptures is still for sale in 1929.

WT 11/1/1929, p. 322

The difference between true and false prophets

WT 5/15/1930, pp. 153–57

27

"Vaccination is a direct violation of the covenant that God made with Noah after the flood."
GOLDEN AGE 2/4/1931, p. 293

"probably some days would be required to make the journey from heaven to earth"
WT 7/1/1931, p. 203

Jehovah's people would now be called "Jehovah's Witnesses."
WT 9/15/1931, p. 279

No question or doubt that Jesus Christ can and does direct every division of his organization, and that he uses holy angels to carry out his orders and direct the course of the remnant.
WT 9/1/1932, p. 263

"There are no Scriptures in God's Word that are contradictory. All are in exact harmony."
WT 2/15/1933, p. 51

Christ Jesus is the head of the organization and it is always the head that directs the operations of the body.
WT 12/1/1933,p 364

If it is difficult to be in harmony with the organization's instructions, you had better check your standing before the Lord.
WT 12/1/1933, p. 364

We should prove by the Word of God whether the things found in *The Watchtower* are from man or from the Lord.
WT 5/1/1934, p. 131

The official organization of Jehovah on earth consists of his anointed remnant and the Jonadabs who walk with the anointed and are to be taught, but not to be leaders.
WT 8/15/1934, p. 249

The press has scoffed at Beth-Sarim, but those faithful men of old will be back on earth before Armageddon ends.
WT 3/15/1937, p. 86

"Jehovah's organization has a visible part on earth which represents the Lord and is under his direct supervision."
WT 5/1/1938, p. 169

"The interpretation of prophecy is not from man but is from Jehovah."
WT 5/1/1938, p. 143

The faithful and wise servant occupies a place similar to that fulfilled by Timothy and Titus; the servant now acts under the direction and supervision of Jesus Christ.

WT 6/1/1938, p. 164

The Lord has perfected and directs his own organization.

WT 6/1/1938, p. 170

The organization is God's and not man's. It is the Lord's representative on earth, and he uses it for his purposes.

WT 6/15/1938, p. 182

Should they marry now? No, is the answer supported by the Scriptures.

WT 11/1/1938, p. 323

There is no reasonable or scriptural injunction to bring children into the world before Armageddon, where we are now.

WT 11/1/1938, p. 324

Romans 10:14–16 refers to Jehovah.

WT 7/1/1940, p. 200

All creatures in heaven and earth shall worship Jesus as he worships the Father.

WT 8/15/1941, p. 252

The new book titled *Children* will prove useful "in the remaining months before Armageddon. . . ."

WT 9/15/1941, p. 288

Spend six hours a day in taking the book *Children* to others. Parents should encourage their children to share in this activity if they would have them live.

WT 9/15/1941, p. 288

The end of Nazi-Fascist hierarchy will come and will mark the end forever of demon rule.

WT 12/15/1941, p. 377

God uses *The Watch Tower* to communicate to his people; it does not consist of men's opinions.

WT 1/1/1942, p. 5

No credit is given to the magazine's publishers but to the Author of the Bible who interprets its prophecies.

WT 4/15/1943, p. 127

The Vatican belittles Bible study by claiming it is the only organization authorized and qualified to interpret the Bible.

WT 7/1/1943, p. 201

"No creature or organization on earth can truly presume to sit as the supreme tribunal of interpretation of the Holy Bible."

WT 7/1/1943, p. 202

Jehovah uses the servant class to publish the interpretation after the supreme court by Christ Jesus reveals it.

WT 7/1/1943, p. 203

The *Watch Tower* reveals direct communications and quotations from Jehovah God.

WT 7/1/1943, p. 205

The governing body is appointed by Jehovah God. Its purpose is to issue directions and spiritual provisions to all God's people.

WT 11/1/1944, p. 330

Mr. Benjamin Wilson, (translator of the *Emphatic Diaglott*) was a Christadelphian and did not believe in the Trinity.

A 11/8/1944, p. 26

The other sheep do not have the standing of sons of his, but the faithful ones will become such after Armageddon.

WT 8/15/1945, p. 253

You must worship and bow down to Jehovah's chief one, namely Jesus Christ.

WT 10/15/1945, p. 313

Jesus Christ was not made a human creature at his resurrection but was made a spirit, which accounts for his invisibility.

WT 4/1/1947, pp. 101–2

"To get one's name written in that Book of Life will depend upon one's works."

WT 7/1/1947, p. 204

Jesus Christ is the head of the servant, the "ruler."

WT 8/1/1950, p. 230

The *Watch Tower* "invites careful and critical examination of its contents in the light of the Scriptures."

WT 8/15/1950, p. 263

Due to conscience, Jehovah's Witnesses refuse military service.

WT 2/1/1951, p. 73

It is not scriptural to speak of Jehovah as being omnipresent.

WT 10/1/1951, p. 607

Meekly go along with the organization. Do not pit human reasoning, sentiment, and personal feelings against the organization.

WT 2/1/1952, p. 80

"Jehovah and Christ direct and correct the slave as needed, not we as individuals."

WT 2/1/1952, p. 79

The men of Sodom will not be resurrected.

WT 6/1/1952, p. 338

"We must hate in the truest sense, which is to regard with extreme and active aversion, to consider as loathsome, odious, filthy, to detest."

WT 10/1/1952, p. 599

". . . if the children are of age, then there can be a departing and a breaking of family ties in a physical way, because the spiritual ties have already snapped."

WT 11/15/1952, p. 703

Should a Witness have business relationships with one who has been disfellowshiped?

WT 12/1/1952, p. 735

Jesus' fleshly body "was disposed of by Jehovah God, dissolved into its constituent elements or atoms."

WT 9/1/1953, p. 518

". . . it would be unwise for us to try to fix God's throne as being at a particular spot in the universe."

WT 11/15/1953, p. 703

No distinct worship is to be rendered to Jesus Christ, now glorified in heaven.

WT 1/1/1954, p. 31

With the Bible alone many parts can be seen, but with the aid of the Watchtower publications a much more complete picture of Jehovah's purposes comes into view.

WT 3/15/1954, p. 164

Clearly the loaf pictures not Jesus' body but his body members, the Christian congregation.

WT 3/15/1954, p. 174

"The Bible is organization-minded and it cannot be fully understood without our having the theocratic organization in mind."

WT 9/1/1954, p. 529

It must have taken Adam quite some time to name all the animals. After Adam completed his work Eve was created.

WT 2/1/1955, p. 95

That remaining one right religion is that of Jehovah's Witnesses. It is not conceited for us to say that.

WT 2/15/1955, p. 124

We are not to look for Christ to be visible to human eyes when he comes again.

WT 2/15/1955, p. 102

The remnant is the channel of communication.

WT 5/15/1955, p. 315

The appointment of all servants in the congregations rests with the governing body of the "faithful and discreet slave" class under the direct supervision of Jesus Christ.

WT 6/1/1955, p. 333

The WT comments on the court case held in Scotland in 1954.

WT 6/1/1955, pp. 329–30

"His body? Yes, his own body, his whole body, head and all that he was to give for them . . . the body with which he next associates his own blood when speaking of the cup. "

WT 1/15/1956, p. 49

"Very plainly the spirits in which ex-priest Greber believes helped him in his translation."

WT 2/15/1956, pp. 110–11

For Jesus to provide the ransom he must be a perfect man—no more, no less.

WT 4/15/1956, p. 239

"But nowhere in the Bible do we find that parents are to be worshiped, or that there should be a Father's Day and a Mother's Day kept in their honor."

A 5/8/1956, p. 25

"In fact, the month of May of Mother's Day is understood to be named after Maia, a demon worshiped by the pagans. . . . 'the fruitful mother'"

A 5/8/1956, p. 25

Newcomers must learn to fall in line with the principles and policies of the New World Society.

WT 6/1/1956, p. 345

Who controls the organization? Jehovah!

WT 11/1/1956, p. 666

The past few decades show Jehovah has been and is using the Watchtower and Jehovah's Witnesses as a teaching organization, the "faithful and discreet slave."

WT 3/15/1957, p. 163

"God has not arranged for that Word to speak independently or to shine forth lifegiving truths by itself. It is through his organization God provides this light."

WT 5/1/1957, p. 274

"The world is full of Bibles. . . . Why then do the people not know which way to go? Because they do not also have the teaching or law of the mother, which is light."

WT 5/1/1957, p. 274

". . . we must recognize not only Jehovah God as our Father but his organization as our Mother."

WT 5/1/1957, p. 274

Do not criticize the organization. If Jehovah permits it, who are we to insist it should be different?

WT 5/1/1957, p. 284

"Did she tell a lie? No, she did not. She was not a liar. Rather, she was using theocratic war strategy, hiding the truth by action and word for the sake of the ministry."

WT 5/1/1957, p. 285

Respond to the directions of the organization as you would the voice of God.

WT 6/15/1957, p. 370

God has set the members in the governing body, each one of them just as He pleased.

WT 7/15/1958, p. 436

A pastor prophesied the end; he was called a false prophet.

WT 10/15/1958, p. 613

Who will be Jehovah's prophet? Who will be the modern Jeremiah? The plain facts show God has been pleased to use Jehovah's Witnesses.

WT 1/15/1959, pp. 40–41

Stephen's prayer to Jesus at Acts 7:59

WT 2/1/1959, p. 96

The one and only true God is Jehovah.

WT 3/1/1959, p. 150

Do not erroneously conclude that Christians are to worship Christ. That is not what the Bible taught.

WT 7/15/1959, p. 421

In due time God exalted Jesus to the highest position a creature could be given.

A 9/22/1959, p. 7

"We avoid all kinds of creature worship and anything that would stimulate to creature worship. . . . The Society does not identify the writers of the various books, booklets, magazines or articles that it publishes."

WT 10/1/1959, p. 607

A Christian must always be part of Jehovah's visible organization.

WT 1/1/1960, p. 19

"This apostasy should not surprise us. . . . Recovery from the apostasy waited until the latter part of the 19th century. At that time a group of Christians gathered for a study of God's Word, divesting themselves of the creedal and sectarian chains of Christendom."

A 2/8/1960, p. 4

"Still there are those who think that they can allow themselves to see association with worldly friends or relatives for entertainment. . . . Rather, 'do not become partners with them . . . and quit sharing with them. . . .'"

WT 2/15/1960, p. 112

Lying to God's enemies is not really lying but war strategy.

WT 6/1/1960, p. 352

34

The slave class is the sole channel of biblical truth.

WT 7/15/1960, p. 439

"When Jesus came to God's spiritual temple in 1918 for the purpose of judging men, Christendom was rejected."

WT 8/1/1960, p. 462

All JWs, though international, are of "one heart and soul," and the same line of thought.

WT 8/1/1960, p. 474

Why should we insist on choosing our own way, setting our own standards or judgments more highly than that of this proved faithful slave?

WT 5/1/1961, p. 274

"in order to hate what is bad a Christian must hate the person"

WT 7/15/1961, p. 420

"If one renders obedient service to someone or some organization, whether willingly or under compulsion, looking up to such as possessing a position of superior rulership and great authority, then that one can Scripturally be said to be a worshiper."

WT 9/1/1961, p. 525

"He wants his earthly servants united, and so he has made understanding the Bible today dependent upon associating with his organization."

WT 11/1/1961, p. 668

"Parents who love their children and who want to see them alive in God's new world will encourage and guide them toward goals of increased service and responsibility."

WT 3/15/1962, p. 179

Johannes Greber cited for support.

WT 9/15/1962, p. 554

"Idolatry . . . is the worship of any one or any thing aside from the true God"

WT 1/15/1963, p. 53

E. C. Colwell quoted

WT 2/1/1963, p. 95

Jehovah is pleased to use the slave class. The chief publication of Bible truth since 1879 is *The Watchtower.*

WT 6/1/1963, p. 338

".. . a disfellowshiped relative who does not live in the same home, contact with him is also kept to what is absolutely necessary . . . even curtailed completely if at all possible."

WT 7/15/1963, p. 443

"We should not see how close we can get to relatives who are disfellowshiped from Jehovah's organization, but we should 'quit mixing in company' with them."

WT 7/15/1963, p. 444

The Scriptures that seem to attribute omnipresence to God must be taken symbolically or figuratively.

A 8/22/1963, p. 28

It is not persecution for an informed person to expose a certain religion as being false.

WT 11/15/1963, p. 688

One of the various ways in which the *New World Translation* honors God is by avoiding trinitarian bias.

WT 12/15/1963, p. 763

"as soon as the first human pair sinned God knew it or learned it"

WT 1/15/1964, p. 52

A pet should not be given a blood transfusion.

WT 2/15/1964, p. 127

Forbidding to marry is wrong.

WT 4/1/1964, p. 199

"It is through the columns of *The Watchtower* that Jehovah provides direction and constant Scriptural counsel to his people. . . ."

WT 5/1/1964, p. 277

Through Jehovah's agency he is having prophesying carried out. Jehovah is behind all of it.

WT 6/15/1964, p. 365

An elderly couple pray before unwrapping each issue of *The Watchtower* that God will make them worthy to see his message.

WT 9/15/1964, p. 574

"God has on earth today a prophetlike organization"

WT 10/1/1964, p. 601

"Christians who associated with this Mr. Russell in proclaiming the end of the Gentile Times and the full establishment of God's kingdom in the heavens were . . . called 'Russellites.'"
WT 11/1/1964, p. 653

". . . it is unscriptural for worshipers of the living and true God to render worship to the Son of God, Jesus Christ."
WT 11/1/1964, p. 671

A true minister of God will welcome a sincere examination of the message that he preaches. The Beroeans set a good example at Acts 17:11. [For the new view of this see WT 2/15/1981, p. 18.]
A 11/22/1964, pp. 5–6

"The best method of proof is to put a prophecy to the test of time and circumstances."
WT 3/1/1965, p. 151

"Jehovah's theocratically controlled organization under the immediate direction of Jehovah God himself"
WT 6/1/1965, p. 352

"the visible governing body made up of those servants whom Jehovah himself would appoint"
WT 6/1/1965, p. 352

"He does not impart his holy spirit and an understanding and appreciation of his Word apart from his visible organization."
WT 7/1/1965, p. 391

The men of Sodom will be resurrected.
WT 8/1/1965, p. 479

Vaccinations appear to have caused a marked decrease in diseases.
A 8/22/1965, p. 20

Jesus had nails in his hands at John 20:19–29.
WT 1/15/1966, p. 63

"Contrary to what some may think, it is not unkind and unloving to lay bare falsehood and corruption."
WT 3/1/1966, p. 132

When? This generation. How much longer? The generation that saw the beginning of the woes in 1914 would see the end.
A 10/8/1966, pp. 17–20

37

"In what year, then, would the first 6,000 years of man's existence and also the first 6,000 years of God's rest day come to an end? The year 1975."

A 10/8/1966, p. 19

Eve could well have been created in the same year as Adam, 4026 B.C.E.

A 10/8/1966, p. 19

"Discussion of 1975 overshadowed about everything else. 'The new book compels us to realize that Armageddon is, in fact, very close indeed,' said a conventioner."

WT 10/15/1966, p. 629

Why Jehovah's Witnesses call at your door.

WT 4/15/1967, p. 227

". . . 1975 marks the end of 6,000 years of human experience. . . . Will it be the time when God executes the wicked? . . . It very well could be, but we will have to wait to see."

WT 5/1/1967, p. 262

"What, can we say, is the basic principle underlying the movement of Jehovah's living organization? It can be expressed in one word: OBEDIENCE."

WT 6/1/1967, p. 337

Heavy research is not necessary. The Watch Tower has done it for you. The most beneficial study you can do is to read *The Watchtower* or *Awake!* or a new book by the organization.

WT 6/1/1967, p. 338

". . . the Bible is an organizational book. . . . For this reason the Bible cannot be properly understood without Jehovah's visible organization in mind."

WT 10/1/1967, p. 587

". . . his sole visible channel, through whom alone spiritual instruction was to come. . . . recognize and accept this appointment of the 'faithful and discreet slave' and be submissive to it."

WT 10/1/1967, p. 590

"Since 1879 the *Watch Tower* magazine has been used by this collective group to dispense spiritual food regularly to those of this 'little flock' of true Christians."

WT 10/1/1967, p. 590

"Make haste to identify the visible theocratic organization of God. . . . It is essential for life. Doing so, be complete in accepting its every aspect. We cannot claim to love God, yet deny his Word and channel of communication."

WT 10/1/1967, p. 591

". . . in submitting to Jehovah's visible theocratic organization, we must be in full and complete agreement with every feature of its apostolic procedure and requirements."

WT 10/1/1967, p. 592

Organ transplants are cannibalism, hence inappropriate for Christians.

WT 11/15/1967, pp. 702–4

Comparison between Jehovah's Witnesses and early Christianity

A 3/22/1968, p. 8

title of article: "Making Wise Use of the Remaining Time"

WT 5/1/1968, p. 270

Naming the animals took a relatively brief period of time after Adam's creation.

WT 5/1/1968, p. 271

". . . it is logical he would create Eve soon after Adam, perhaps just a few weeks or months later in the same year, 4026 B.C.E."

WT 5/1/1968, p. 271

". . . the autumn of 1975, fully 6,000 years into God's seventh day, his rest day."

WT 5/1/1968, p. 271

"Does this mean that the year 1975 will bring the battle of Armageddon? No one can say with certainty what any particular year will bring."

WT 5/1/1968, pp. 272–73

Jehovah God has commissioned his "faithful and discreet slave" to dispense spiritual food at the proper time. They publish *The Watchtower.*

WT 5/1/1968, p. 279

Jehovah's Witnesses consider *all* organ transplants to be cannibalism, hence unacceptable.

A 6/8/1968, p. 21

title of article: "Why Are You Looking Forward to 1975?"
WT 8/15/1968, p. 494

"Are we to assume from this study that the battle of Armageddon will be all over by the autumn of 1975, and the long-looked-for thousand-year reign of Christ will begin by then? Possibly. . . . It may involve only a difference of weeks or months, not years."
WT 8/15/1968, p. 499

"Adam and Eve were created in 4026 B.C.E."
A 10/8/1968, p. 14

"True, there have been those in times past who predicted an 'end to the world,' even announcing a specific date. . . . The 'end' did not come. They were guilty of false prophesying. . . . Missing from such people were God's truths and the evidence that he was guiding and using them."
A 10/8/1968, p. 23

"Jesus was obviously speaking about those who were old enough to witness *with understanding* what took place when the 'last days' began. . . . Even if we presume that youngsters 15 years of age would be perceptive enough to realize the import of what happened in 1914, it would still make the youngest of 'this generation' nearly 70 years old today. . . . Jesus said that the end of this wicked world would come *before* that generation passed away in death."
A 10/8/1968, p. 13

"Hence, the first six thousand years since man's creation could be likened to the first six days of the week in ancient Israel. The seventh one-thousand-year period could be likened to the seventh day, the sabbath, of that week.—2 Pet. 3:8 How fitting it would be for God, following this pattern, to end man's misery after six thousand years of human rule and follow it with His glorious Kingdom rule for a thousand years!"
A 10/8/1968, p. 14

"Does this mean that the above evidence positively points to 1975 as the time for the complete end of this system of things? Since the Bible does not specifically state this, no man can say. . . . If the 1970's should see intervention by Jehovah God to bring an end to a corrupt world drifting toward ultimate disintegration, that should surely not surprise us."
A 10/8/1968, p. 14

heading of chronological chart: "6,000 Years of Human History Ending in 1975"

A 10/8/1968, p. 15

"Thus the Scriptures and sound reasoning make clear that Satan is a real, live person in the invisible realm. He was, and is, a historical person, an actual living creature."

WT 12/1/1968, p. 708

". . . because it means 'Anointed One' . . . Jesus could not bear the title 'Christ' until . . . his baptism. . . ."

WT 1/1/1969, p. 29

"Jesus foretold that . . . there would be a 'faithful and discreet slave' acting as his channel of communication"

WT 1/15/1969, p. 51

Bridal veil and white dress have possible pagan origins.

WT 1/15/1969, p. 60

Do not pursue higher education. There is very little time left! Make pioneer service, the full-time ministry with the possibility of Bethel or missionary service, your goal.

WT 3/15/1969, p. 171

"Jehovah's organization . . . should influence our every decision."

WT 3/15/1969, p. 172

"There is Scriptural evidence for concluding that Michael was the name of Jesus Christ before he left heaven and after his return."

WT 5/15/1969, p. 307

Since there is such a short time left, study no longer than six months with a prospective convert.

WT 5/15/1969, p. 312

Recently researchers of the Bible have rechecked its chronology and found that man's first 6,000 years will end in the mid-seventies—a fitting time for Jehovah to usher in a sabbath millennium for his creatures.

WT 10/15/1969, pp. 622–23

In the *Kingdom Interlinear Translation* we want the original Greek, whether it agrees literally with the New World Translation or not.

WT 11/15/1969, p. 692

The trinity is a basic false doctrine.
WT 4/1/1970, p. 210

". . . adhering to false religion can mean your eternal destruction. . . . Are true Christians going to stand by quietly and say nothing about such gross misrepresentations? Hardly!"
WT 4/15/1970, p. 246

"How should a faithful Christian act toward a relative outside the immediate family circle who has been disfellowshiped? . . . [contact with] one who does not live in the same household . . . would be much more rare than between persons living in the same home. Yet there might be some absolutely necessary family matters requiring communication, such as legalities over a will or property."
WT 6/1/1970, pp. 351–52

"Christians rightly hate those who are confirmed enemies of God, such as the devil and his demons, as well as men who have deliberately and knowingly taken their stand against Jehovah."
WT 11/15/1970, p. 695

"Can it be stated flatly that only baptized Witnesses of Jehovah will survive Armageddon?" Yes, with a few exceptions.
WT 1/15/1971, p. 63

The Bible should be our primary textbook for study.
WT 4/15/1971, p. 230

"'. . . an idolatrous symbol.' . . . There are Christians today who feel similarly regarding national flags. They are Jehovah's Witnesses. . . . they decline to participate in flag ceremonies."
A 9/8/1971, p. 14

". . . idolatrous worshipers of a man-made organization . . ."
WT 12/1/1971, p. 723

Jehovah's Witness organizational chart
WT 12/1/1971, p. 749

We have the proof more than ever before that God enthroned his Son in 1914, and that we are now in the "time of the end."
WT 12/15/1971, p. 753

"It is a theocratic organization, ruled from the divine Top down, and not from the rank and file up."
WT 12/15/1971, p. 754

Wedding ring has possible pagan origins.
WT 1/15/1972, p. 63

Was there a group that Jehovah would commission to speak as a prophet like Ezekiel?
WT 3/15/1972, p. 189

"This 'prophet' was not one man, but was a body of men and women. It was the small group of footstep followers of Jesus Christ, known at that time as International Bible Students. Today they are known as Jehovah's Christian witnesses."
WT 4/1/1972, p. 197

"Of course, it is easy to say that this group acts as a 'prophet' of God. It is another thing to prove it. The only way that this can be done is to review the record."
WT 4/1/1972, p. 197

"under angelic direction"
WT 4/1/1972, p. 200

Accept willingly the counsel provided through the printed page.
WT 5/1/1972, p. 272

A. T. Robertson, a prominent Greek grammarian, quoted
A 5/22/1972, p. 28

The organization is controlled altogether by God and by the forces he operates.
WT 8/1/1972, p. 458

"Through the columns of *The Watchtower* comes increased light on God's Word as Jehovah makes it known."
WT 8/1/1972, p. 460

"Working hard for the reward of eternal life"
WT 8/15/1972, p. 491

"No biblical evidence even intimates that Jesus died on a cross."
A 11/8/1972, p. 28

Certain specific forms of contact are ruled improper between husband and wife in the marriage bed. Married couples must avoid these practices; otherwise, they may be disfellowshiped by the elders.
WT 12/1/1972, pp. 734–36

"Micah proved to be a true prophet of the one true God, meeting the three basic requirements . . . (1) He spoke in the name of the true God, (2) His prophecies came true. . . ."

WT 12/15/1972, p. 743

"So, recognition of that governing body and its place in God's theocratic arrangement of things is necessary for submission to the headship of God's Son."

WT 12/15/1972, p. 755

Old baptism questions (For new questions see WT 6/1/1985.)

WT 5/1/1973, p. 280

"They may now be given a reasonable period of time, such as six months, in which to free themselves of the addiction [smoking]."

WT 6/1/1973, p. 340

"Jehovah's organization alone, in all the earth, is directed by God's holy spirit or active force."

WT 7/1/1973, p. 402

The Bible is a sealed book except to the organization.

WT 7/1/1973, p. 402

"*Zion's Watch Tower* of March 1880 had declared: '"The Times of the Gentiles" extend to 1914, and the heavenly kingdom will not have full sway till then.' Only God by his holy spirit could have revealed this to those early Bible students so far in advance."

WT 7/1/1973, p. 402

"How very much true Christians appreciate associating with the only organization on earth that understands the 'deep things of God'!"

WT 7/1/1973, p. 402

"That same holy spirit and angelic direction still affect the preaching activities of Christian ministers."

WT 7/1/1973, p. 405

"Jesus could not have ascended to heaven forty days after his resurrection had he been raised as a human of flesh and blood."

A 7/22/1973, p. 4

Jesus must be a spirit being. He simply materialized bodies.

A 7/22/1973, p. 4

44

"Yes, we should be deeply appreciative of all the fine spiritual food that the 'faithful and discreet slave' class has been providing through *The Watchtower*, now for ninety-four years."
WT 8/1/1973, p. 460

". . . the generation alive in 1914, some will see the major fulfillment of Christ Jesus' prophecy and the destruction. . . ."
A 10/8/1973, p. 19

Examine the evidence. Reasonable persons want to examine both sides of a matter. That is how one arrives at the truth.
A 10/22/1973, p. 6

"Is the Devil a personification or a person? . . . Can an unintelligent 'force' carry on a conversation with a person? . . . only an intelligent person could. . . . 'Every quality, every action, which can indicate personality, is attributed to him in language which cannot be explained away.'"
A 12/8/1973, p. 27

Can you be true to God and hide the facts?
WT 1/15/1974, p. 35

When persons are being misled we should warn them; they may resent it, but that does not free us from the moral responsibility to give warning.
WT 1/15/1974, p. 35

title of article: "Does Christianity Require Belief in a Trinity?"
WT 2/1/1974, p. 75

"The ideal situation is for parents to have such a fine program outlined for their children that little or no time remains for outside associations."
WT 2/1/1974, p. 93

Picture of Jesus with one nail through both hands
A 4/8/1974, p. 14

"Similarly the 'false prophet' is not a person, but is a system or an organization."
WT 6/15/1974, p. 381

"It also tells us that this millennium must be preceded immediately by the most destructive war in all human history. We can now see the political rulers . . . being gathered . . . for that War of all wars. . . ."
WT 7/1/1974, p. 397

45

"There is, however, nothing to show that Jews with a balanced and Scriptural viewpoint would refuse to greet a 'man of the nations' or a tax collector. Jesus' counsel about greetings, in connection with his exhortation to imitate God in his undeserved kindness toward 'wicked people and good,' would seem to rule against such a rigid stand."

WT 8/1/1974, pp. 464–65

". . . if a disfellowshiped parent goes to visit a son or daughter or to see grandchildren . . . this is not the concern of the elders. Such a one has a natural right to visit his blood relatives and his offspring."

WT 8/1/1974, p. 471

"When sons or daughters render honor to a parent, though disfellowshiped, by calling to see how such a one's physical health is, or what needs he or she may have, this act in itself is not a spiritual fellowshiping."

WT 8/1/1974, p. 471

"So, the evidence indicates that Jesus did not die on the traditional cross."

A 9/22/1974, p. 28

"The publications of Jehovah's Witnesses have shown that, according to Bible chronology, it appears that 6,000 years of man's existence will be completed in the mid-1970's. But these publications have never said that the world's end would come then. Nevertheless, there has been considerable individual speculation on the matter."

WT 10/15/1974, p. 635

A great crowd of people are confident that great destruction is imminent, which has been a major factor in their decision not to have children.

A 11/8/1974, p. 11

"Thus the Father alone is THE God, the Supreme One, to whom all owe worship and to whom all, including the Son, are rightly subject."

WT 3/15/1975, p. 174

Six thousand years of human history will end in September . . . but there is a short time interval between Adam's creation and that of Eve.

WT 5/1/1975, p. 285

46

Why some sins are not forgiven.

WT 8/1/1975, p. 459

The resurrected body of Christ—was it flesh and blood?

WT 8/1/1975, p. 478

". . . Jehovah God disposed of the sacrificed body of his Son."

WT 8/1/1975, p. 479

Should you defend yourself? A homeowner has the right to inflict hard blows. Jesus' apostles had at least two swords.

A 9/8/1975, pp. 27–28

". . . the Bible record shows . . . a time lapse between the creation of Adam and that of his wife, Eve. . . . Whether that period amounted to weeks or months or years, we do not know. So we do not know exactly when Jehovah's great 'rest day' began, nor do we know exactly when it will end. The same applies to the beginning of Christ's millennial reign."

WT 10/1/1975, p. 579

Johannes Greber quoted about Matthew 27:52–53

WT 10/15/1975, p. 640

Watchtower's answer for John 1:1

WT 11/15/1975, p. 702

The time of Adam's creation can be determined, but the beginning of God's rest day cannot because there was a time lapse of unspecified length between Adam's creation and the creation of Eve.

WT 1/1/1976, p. 30

As of May 1974, more than 2000 had been disfellowshiped for not quitting the unclean practice of smoking.

WT 2/15/1976, p. 123

Failure to respond to the direction of the organization indicates a rejection of Divine rulership.

WT 2/15/1976, p. 124

Johannes Greber cited for support.

WT 4/15/1976, p. 231

Jehovah's Witnesses are not infallible or inspired prophets.

WT 5/15/1976, p. 297

Christians cannot be wishy-washy, going back to the same teachings they had rejected earlier.

WT 5/15/1976, p. 298

"But it is not advisable for us to set our sights on a certain date. . . . If anyone has been disappointed through not following this line of thought, he should now concentrate on adjusting his viewpoint, seeing that it was not the word of God that failed or deceived him and brought disappointment, but that his own understanding was based on wrong premises."
WT 7/15/1976, p. 441

". . . the 'servant' or 'slave' that Jesus foretold must be the members of *spiritual* Israel on earth—not an individual person, but a *body.*"
WT 7/15/1976, p. 443

Christendom borrows from Plato ideas about Christ and the Trinity.
A 8/22/1976, pp. 23–26

Religious symbols to avoid; the cross
A 12/22/1976, pp. 12–15

Chart showing Jehovah God, Jesus Christ, and faithful and discreet slave class
WT 1/1/1977, p. 16

". . . salvation can only be gained by . . . accepting Jesus Christ as the Son of God through whose sacrificial death salvation from sin and death was made possible."
A 1/8/1977, p. 27

In Romans 10:12 the identity of the "Lord" cannot be established with certainty from the context.
WT 2/1/1977, p. 95

William Barclay quoted from *Many Witnesses, One Lord*
WT 5/15/1977, p. 320

God has authorized governmental superior authorities to execute criminals.
A 7/22/1977, p. 7

"Frederick W. Franz . . . an eminent Bible scholar"
WT 8/1/1977, p. 463

Romans 10:13 is referring to Jesus.
WT 5/1/1978, p. 12

There are various publications exposing Jehovah's Witnesses as heretics. We are not afraid of this.
WT 8/1/1978, p. 12

"Jehovah's Witnesses usually present their views in a talk, then open the meeting to questions."

A 8/22/1978, p. 7

Revelation 22:12 is referring to Jehovah.

A 8/22/1978, p. 28

Revelation 22:7, 12, 20 is referring to Jesus.

WT 10/1/1978, p. 15

"Thus, when it comes to the application in our time, the 'generation' logically would not apply to babies born during World War I."

WT 10/1/1978, p. 31

The Trinity is a doctrine of Platonic origin.

WT 10/15/1978, p. 32

The fruits in Matthew 7:20 include teachings.

WT 11/15/1978, p. 31

". . . Jehovah's Witnesses may not become members of the YMCA . . . "

WT 1/1/1979, p. 30

". . . the great tribulation may not have come as soon as many of us had expected. . . . It draws closer with each day."

WT 2/1/1979, p. 24

"Put faith in a victorious organization!"

WT 3/1/1979, p. 1

title of article: "To Whom Shall We Go but Jesus Christ?"

WT 3/1/1979, p. 20

"Outside the true Christian congregation what alternative organization is there? Only Satan's organization. . . ."

WT 3/1/1979, p. 24

"Jesus is the mediator only for anointed Christians. . . . The 'great crowd' . . . is not in that new covenant."

WT 4/1/1979, p. 31

". . . the invisible 'presence,' or parousia, of the glorified Jesus Christ began at the end of the Gentile Times in 1914."

WT 6/15/1979, p. 27

title of article: "Keeping Watch for 100 Years"

WT 7/1/1979, p. 4

"Jesus was dead, he was unconscious, out of existence. Death did not mean a transition to another life for Jesus; rather, nonexistence."

A 7/22/1979, p. 27

Those who forbid marriage have departed from the faith.

WT 9/15/1979, p. 31

". . . by the time she was five, on her own she would go from house to house and offer *The Watchtower* and *Awake!*"

WT 10/15/1979, p. 24

"To keep in relationship with 'our Savior, God,' the 'great crowd' needs to remain united with the remnant of spiritual Israelites."

WT 11/15/1979, p. 27

"What, then, is Christ's role in this program of salvation? . . . 'There is one God, and one mediator between God and men [not, *all* men], a man Christ Jesus.'"

WT 11/15/1979, p. 26

"Jesus was not born on December 25th. . . . Hence, celebrating his birthday through Christmas observance on December 25 is totally inappropriate for those guided by the Holy Scriptures."

WT 12/15/1979, p. 5

Romans 10:13 is referring to Jehovah.

WT 2/1/1980, p. 16

"Considerable expectation was aroused regarding the year 1975. . . . Statements published that implied that such realization of hopes by that year was more of a probability than a mere possibility. It is to be regretted . . . *the publication of the information* that contributed to the buildup of hopes centered on that date."

WT 3/15/1980, p. 17

Organ transplants are not necessarily cannibalistic.

WT 3/15/1980, p. 31

Romans 13:1 refers to governments.

WT 5/15/1980, p. 4

". . . an apostate . . . thinks he knows better than his fellow Christians, better also than the 'faithful and discreet slave,' through whom he has learned the best part, if not all that he knows about Jehovah God and his purposes."

WT 8/1/1980, pp. 19–20

"It is the generation of people who saw the catastrophic events that broke forth in connection with World War I from 1914 onward. . . . If you assume that 10 is the age at which an event creates a lasting impression . . ."

WT 10/15/1980, p. 31

"God being an individual, a Person with a spirit body, has a place where he resides, and so he could not be at any other place at the same time."

WT 2/15/1981, p. 6

Jehovah caused the Bible to be written in such a way that you need his human channel to understand it.

WT 2/15/1981, p. 17

A new view of the Beroeans, Acts 17:11—They wanted to have this good news prove true. (For the old view, see *Awake!* magazine, 11/22/1964, pp. 5–6.)

WT 2/15/1981, p. 18

"The brothers preparing these publications are not infallible."

WT 2/15/1981, p. 19

"We all need help to understand the Bible, and we cannot find the Scriptural guidance we need outside the 'faithful and discreet slave' organization."

WT 2/15/1981, p. 19

"At the Brooklyn headquarters . . . there are more mature Christian elders, both of the 'remnant' and of the 'other sheep,' than anywhere else upon earth."

WT 2/15/1981, p. 19

"Jehovah is not pleased if we receive that food as though it might contain something harmful. We should have confidence in the channel God is using."

WT 2/15/1981, p. 19

". . . *The Watchtower* and its companion magazine *Awake!* (formerly *The Golden Age,* then *Consolation*). These Bible-based periodicals . . ."

WT 3/1/1981, p. 18

"Indeed, this 'slave,' or spirit-anointed congregation, is the one approved channel representing God's kingdom on earth."

WT 3/1/1981, p. 24

Your attitude toward the anointed is the determining factor whether you go into everlasting cutting off or everlasting life.

WT 8/1/1981, p. 26

Answer to *Ha-Adon* at Romans 10:9

WT 8/1/1981, p. 31

". . . from among the ranks of Jehovah's people . . . haughty ones . . . say that it is sufficient to read the Bible exclusively, either alone or in small groups at home. But, strangely, through such 'Bible reading,' they have reverted right back to the apostate doctrines that commentaries by Christendom's clergy were teaching 100 years ago. . . ."

WT 8/15/1981, pp. 28–29

"Persons who make themselves 'not of our sort' by deliberately rejecting the faith and beliefs of Jehovah's Witnesses should appropriately be viewed and treated as are those who have been disfellowshiped for wrongdoing."

WT 9/15/1981, p. 23

"Would upholding God's righteousness and his disfellowshiping arrangement mean that a Christian should not speak at all with an expelled person, not even saying 'Hello'? . . . a simple 'Hello' to someone can be the first step that develops into a conversation. . . . Why do Christians not greet or speak with disfellowshiped persons?"

WT 9/15/1981, pp. 24–26

"Christians related to such a disfellowshiped person living outside the home should strive to avoid needless association, even keeping business dealings to a minimum."

WT 9/15/1981, p. 29

Those who desire life in the New Order must come into a right relationship with the organization.

WT 11/15/1981, pp. 16–17

". . . come to Jehovah's organization for salvation . . ."

WT 11/15/1981, p. 21

"What is your attitude toward directives from 'the faithful and discreet slave'? Loyalty should move you to be 'ready to obey.'"

WT 12/1/1981, p. 14

"At times explanations given by Jehovah's visible organization have shown adjustments, seemingly to previous points of view. But this has not actually been the case. . . . 'Tacking' into the wind . . ."

WT 12/1/1981, p. 27

"Unless we are in touch with this channel of communication that God is using, we will not progress along the road to life, no matter how much Bible reading we do."

WT 12/1/1981, p. 27

". . . of course, such development of understanding, involving 'tacking' as it were, has often served as a test of loyalty for those associated with the 'faithful and discreet slave' . . . invariably an improved position results."

WT 12/1/1981, p. 31

"Apart from this, the only choice is association with Satan's political 'wild beast' and 'Babylon the Great,' the world empire of false religion."

WT 12/1/1981, p. 31

"Favored indeed are all those who serve loyally with the 'faithful and discreet slave' organization, Jehovah's visible agent of communication!"

WT 12/1/1981, p. 31

"In order to rise again to life, a person must first be dead, for life is the opposite of death."

WT 12/15/1981, pp. 16–17

". . . the heavenly hope was held out, highlighted and stressed until about the year 1935. Then as 'light flashed up' to reveal clearly the identity of the 'great crowd' of Revelation 7:9, the emphasis began to be placed on the earthly hope."

WT 2/1/1982, p. 28

"However, though leeches parasitically feed on blood in their natural state at present, it would not be proper for a Christian to permit leeches to draw his blood. . . . [That] would involve deliberately feeding blood to these creatures. That would conflict with the Bible's indication that blood, being sacred and representing life, should be disposed of if it is removed from a body."

WT 6/15/1982, p. 31

Illustration from liquor company ad used as *Watchtower* cover illustration; compare individual magazine with bound volume where a different illustration was substituted after legal maneuvering.

WT 9/15/1982, p. 1

". . . the 'prophet' whom Jehovah has raised up has been, not an individual man as in the case of Jeremiah, but a class."

WT 10/1/1982, p. 27

Jehovah's Witnesses entertained the "one hope" of Ephesians 4:4–6 until 1935; since 1935 they have published the earthly hope.

WT 12/15/1982, p. 19

"Under angelic direction . . . Jehovah's Witnesses today have 'everlasting good news to declare.'"

WT 12/15/1982, pp. 24–25

"Avoid independent thinking . . . questioning the counsel that is provided by God's visible organization."

WT 1/15/1983, p. 22

"Fight against independent thinking."

WT 1/15/1983, p. 27

". . . yet there are some who point out that the organization has had to make adjustments before, and so they argue: 'This shows that we have to make up our own mind on what to believe.' This is independent thinking. Why is it so dangerous? Such thinking is an evidence of pride."

WT 1/15/1983, p. 27

"To receive everlasting life in the earthly Paradise we must identify that organization and serve God as part of it."

WT 2/15/1983, p. 12

Four requirements to reside forever on paradise earth

WT 2/15/1983, pp. 12–13

"In Hebrews 1:6 the Greek word *proskynéo* may mean: 1. Rendering respectful obeisance, as 'bowing down,' to Jesus as the one whom Jehovah God has honored and glorified 2. Worshiping Jehovah God through or by means of his chief representative, his Son Jesus."

WT 2/15/1983, p. 18

Read only the Bible? Christendom does this and look at the misunderstanding of the true message of God's Word!

WT 3/1/1983, p. 25

"an organization to direct the minds of God's people"

WT 3/1/1983, p. 25

Illustration of "other sheep" looking at the "little flock" who, in turn, are looking at Christ

WT 3/15/1983, p. 9

"Why, in recent years, has *The Watchtower* not made use of the translation by the former Catholic priest, Johannes Greber? . . . *The Watchtower* has deemed it improper to make use of a translation that has such a close rapport with spiritism."

WT 4/1/1983, p. 31

"Was 'the Word' God? . . . Its correct rendering is: '. . . the Word was a god.'"

WT 12/1/1983, p. 14

"We all need to face up to the fact that Christmas and its music are not from Jehovah, the God of truth. Then what is their source? . . . Satan the Devil."

WT 12/15/1983, p. 7

"Yes, Satan the Devil can ingeniously make Christmas music appear to be of God and the singing of it a Christian duty that honors Him and his Son. In reality, it does just the opposite."

WT 12/15/1983, p. 7

"What outstanding truths were made known in 1925? . . . the prophecies showing that God's promised kingdom had been born in the heavens in 1914."

WT 1/1/1984, p. 10

Does it matter what you believe about Jesus? Yes!

WT 2/1/1984, p. 3

title of article: "The Trinity—Should You Believe It?"

WT 2/1/1984, p. 4

"Does not the Bible show that some people will go to heaven? Yes, the Bible does teach that a limited number go to heaven for a special reason."

WT 2/15/1984, p. 4

"So, it would be foolhardy, as well as a waste of valuable time, for Jehovah's Witnesses to accept and expose themselves to false religious literature that is designed to deceive."

WT 5/1/1984, p. 31

"If Jesus used 'generation' in that sense and we apply it to 1914, then the babies of that generation are now 70 years old or older. . . . Some of them 'will by no means pass away until all things occur.'"

WT 5/15/1984, p. 5

Encyclopedia quotes about the Trinity

WT 8/1/1984, pp. 21–22

Regarding the Roman Catholic Church: Any organization that claims to be the way of salvation should be willing to submit to scrutiny and criticism.

A 8/22/1984, p. 28

title of article: "An Open or a Closed Mind?—Which Do You Have?"

A 11/22/1984, pp. 3–4

"'Michael the great prince' is none other than Jesus Christ himself.—Daniel 12:1"

WT 12/15/1984, p. 29

"God has arranged for the 'good news of the kingdom' to be proclaimed so that each individual will have opportunity to work out his own salvation."

WT 2/1/1985, p. 5

"There is only a remnant of such spiritual sons now living, and these are the ones who properly partake of the emblems. This, then, accounts for the vast majority of Jehovah's Witnesses being observers and not partakers."

WT 2/15/1985, p. 17

"Before the 1914 generation completely dies out, God's judgment must be executed."

WT 5/1/1985, p. 4

New questions for baptismal candidates (See WT 5/1/1973 for old questions.)

WT 6/1/1985, p. 30

". . . to rely simply on personal Bible reading and interpretation is to become like a solitary tree in a parched land."

WT 6/1/1985, p. 20

"We must not lose sight of the fact that God is directing his organization."

WT 6/1/1985, p. 19

". . . the footnotes in *Watchtower* articles, some of which refer the reader to an older publication . . . locate that older publication and then . . . the pages referred to."

WT 6/15/1985, p. 12

The great crowd is tested as to the people's integrity, their continued faithfulness. The final test will result in Jehovah declaring them righteous.

WT 10/15/1985, p. 31

The "other sheep" have a relatively righteous standing.

WT 12/1/1985, p. 17

"Shocking as it is, even some who have been prominent in Jehovah's organization have succumbed to immoral practices, including homosexuality, wife swapping, and child molesting."

WT 1/1/1986, p. 13

"He said: 'Unless anyone is born again, he cannot see the kingdom of God.' (John 3:3–5) . . . The 'other sheep' do not need any such rebirth, for their goal is life everlasting in the restored earthly Paradise as subjects of the Kingdom."

WT 2/15/1986, p. 14

"Who, then, may properly partake of . . . the bread and the wine? . . . Those of the 'other sheep' class are not in the new covenant and so do not partake."

WT 2/15/1986, p. 15

"Do you wisely destroy apostate material?"

WT 3/15/1986, p. 12

"Why is reading apostate publications similar to reading pornographic literature?"

WT 3/15/1986, p. 14

"If you are counseled or even reproved for some wrong practice or attitude, this, too, may prove to be an ideal time for the Devil to prompt you to ask yourself if you are in the right organization."

WT 3/15/1986, p. 16

"Beware of those who try to put forward their own contrary opinions."

WT 3/15/1986, p. 17

"Some opposers claim that Jehovah's Witnesses are false prophets. These opponents say that dates have been set, but nothing has happened. Again we ask, What is the motive of these critics?"

WT 3/15/1986, p. 19

". . . the need to revise our understanding somewhat does not make us false prophets."

WT 3/15/1986, p. 19

Association with JWs requires accepting the teachings of the Bible, including scriptural beliefs that are unique to Jehovah's Witnesses.

WT 4/1/1986, p. 31

"God has on earth a people, all of whom are prophets, or witnesses for God . . . Jehovah's Witnesses."

A 6/8/1986, p. 9

"How could Jesus be 'a god' . . . ?"

WT 7/1/1986, p. 31

"The title *ho theos* [the God, or God] . . . is not applied in the N[ew] T[estament] to Jesus. . . ." [Editor's note: See John 20:28, where *ho theos* is applied to Jesus.]

WT 7/1/1986, p. 31

Pinchas Lapide quoted about the resurrection of Jesus

WT 8/15/1986, p. 19

If a JW joins another religion, an announcement is made to the congregation to stop associating with him.

WT 10/15/1986, p. 31

Awake! discontinues statements in masthead about the generation that saw 1914.

A 1/8/1987, p. 4

"So, all who desire to be acquainted with true prophecy and to practice true religion need to turn to the Bible."
WT 5/1/1987, p. 6

The autobiography of Frederick W. Franz
WT 5/1/1987, pp. 22–30

". . . we cannot hope to receive holy spirit if we ignore the earthly channel Jehovah is using today. . . ."
WT 7/15/1987, pp. 18–19

"Jesus most likely was executed on an upright stake without any crossbeam. No man today can know with certainty even how many nails were used in Jesus' case."
WT 8/15/1987, p. 29

title of article: "Is Your Giving a Sacrifice? A Balanced View of Contributions"
WT 12/1/1987, pp. 28–31

title of article: "The Bible's Viewpoint—Who Are 'Born Again'?"
A 2/8/1988, pp. 26–27

Awake! magazine resumes statements in masthead about the generation that saw 1914.
A 3/8/1988, p. 4

Illustration of Witnesses in 1938 carrying signs denouncing false religion: "Religion is a snare and a racket," "Face the facts"
WT 4/1/1988, p. 16

"Christendom's TV preachers lull millions into believing that they are 'saved' or 'born again.'"
WT 4/1/1988, p. 18

Only a limited number are born again. The great crowd does not need to be born again. Their life is earthly, not heavenly.
WT 4/1/1988, p. 18

". . . a peaceful and secure new world before the generation that saw the events of 1914 passes away."
A 4/8/1988, p. 4

"The Hebrews . . . reckon seventy-five years as one generation. . . ."
A 4/8/1988, p. 14

"Most of the generation of 1914 has passed away. However, there are still millions on earth who were born in that year or prior to it. . . . Jesus' words will come true, 'this generation will not pass away until all these things have happened.'"

WT 4/8/1988, p. 14

The men of Sodom will not be resurrected.

WT 6/1/1988, p. 31

"But separation is allowable if an unbelieving mate's opposition (perhaps including physical restraint) makes it genuinely impossible to pursue true worship and imperils the believer's spirituality."

WT 11/1/1988, p. 22

". . . if a baptized marriage partner acts like an apostate and tries to prevent his mate from serving Jehovah, the elders should handle matters. . . . a legal separation would not be going against Paul's counsel about taking a believer to court."

WT 11/1/1988, p. 23

". . . he may turn in a field service report and a Congregation's Publisher Record card will be made out in his name. This will demonstrate his affiliation with the theocratic organization of Jehovah's Witnesses and his submission to it."

WT 11/15/1988, p. 17

"Previously, unbaptized ones who unrepentantly sinned were completely avoided. . . . The Bible does not require that Witnesses avoid speaking with him, for he is not disfellowshipped."

WT 11/15/1988, p. 19

"He [the apostle Paul] was also laying a foundation for a work that would be completed in our 20th century."

WT 1/1/1989, original magazine, p. 12

"He [the apostle Paul] was also laying a foundation for a work that would be completed in our day."

WT 1/1/1989, bound volume, p. 12

"In the early part of our 20th century prior to 1919, the Bible Students, as Jehovah's Witnesses were then known, had to be released from a form of spiritual captivity to the ideas and practices of false religion. . . . Some were exalting creatures, indulging in a personality cult that focused on Charles T. Russell. . . ."

WT 5/1/1989, p. 4

Subject Listing

Apostates

"The endeavor to compel all men to think alike on all subjects, culminated in the great apostasy and the development of the great Papal system. . . ."

WT 9/1/1893, p. 1572

"Rather we should seek for dependent Bible study, rather than for independent Bible study."

WT 9/15/1911, p. 4885

"Any class leader who would make objection to a reference being made to *The Watch Tower* or to *Studies in the Scriptures* in connection with the discussion of any topic should properly be viewed with suspicion as a teacher."

WT 9/15/1911, p. 4885

"Not all of those who were brought into God's family will constitute a part of his official organization."

PROPHECY, p. 84

". . . an apostate . . . thinks he knows better than his fellow Christians, better also than the 'faithful and discreet slave,' through whom he has learned the best part, if not all that he knows about Jehovah God and his purposes."

WT 8/1/1980, pp. 19–20

"... from among the ranks of Jehovah's people ... haughty ones ... say that it is sufficient to read the Bible exclusively, either alone or in small groups at home. But, strangely, through such 'Bible reading,' they have reverted right back to the apostate doctrines that commentaries by Christendom's clergy were teaching 100 years ago. ..."

WT 8/15/1981, pp. 28–29

"Do you wisely destroy apostate material?"

WT 3/15/1986, p. 12

"Why is reading apostate publications similar to reading pornographic literature?"

WT 3/15/1986, p. 14

"Beware of those who try to put forward their own contrary opinions."

WT 3/15/1986, p. 17

Attacking the Church

To understand 1874 one must be spiritually minded, and the clergy is not.

CREATION, p. 291

The clergy ridiculed us because of 1914.

LIGHT, Vol. 1, p. 194

Christendom: spiritual fornicators

LIGHT, Vol. 1, p. 325

An attack against all organized religion; Roman Catholic Church singled out

DEFENDING, p. 60

"When Jesus came to God's spiritual temple in 1918 for the purpose of judging men, Christendom was rejected."

WT 8/1/1960, p. 462

"M'Clintock and Strong's Cyclopoedia, Volume II, page 386, says ... 'As the Roman hierarchy was developed, the clergy came to ... be recognized as the only priesthood and the essential means of communication between man and God.'"

1000 YEARS, pp. 377–78

"Outside the true Christian congregation what alternative organization is there? Only Satan's organization. . . ."

WT 3/1/1979, p. 24

Read only the Bible? Christendom does this and look at the misunderstanding of the true message of God's Word!

WT 3/1/1983, p. 25

Baptism

Old baptismal questions: "(1) Have you repented of your sins and turned around, recognizing yourself before Jehovah God as a condemned sinner who needs salvation, and have you acknowledged that this salvation proceeds from him, the Father, through his Son Jesus Christ? (2) On the basis of this faith in God and in his provision for salvation, have you dedicated yourself unreservedly to God to do his will henceforth as he reveals it to you through Jesus Christ and through the Bible under the enlightening power of the holy spirit?"

WT 5/1/1973, p. 280

New baptismal questions: "(1) On the basis of the sacrifice of Jesus Christ, have you repented of your sins and dedicated yourself to Jehovah to do his will? (2) Do you understand that your dedication and baptism identify you as one of Jehovah's Witnesses in association with God's spirit-directed organization?"

WT 6/1/1985, p. 30

Beth-Sarim

Beth-Sarim was built in 1929 as proof that the resurrection would soon take place.

SALVATION, p. 311

The press has scoffed at Beth-Sarim, but those faithful men of old will be back on earth before Armageddon ends.

WT 3/15/1937, p. 86

Beth-Sarim discussed

CONSOLATION 5/27/1942, p. 3

Beth-Sarim, built in 1930, is now held in trust for the occupancy of those princes on their return.

NEW WORLD, p. 104

Beth-Sarim was built for Brother Rutherford's use.

1975 YEARBOOK, p. 194

Bible Interpreter

New light never contradicts old light, but adds to it.

WT 2/1881, p. 188

"Bible classes and Bible studies all to no purpose until the Lord, in due time, sent them the 'Bible keys,' through the Society"

WT 10/1/1909, p. 4482

"If the six volumes of SCRIPTURE STUDIES are practically the Bible topically arranged, with Bible proof-texts given, we might not improperly name the volumes—the Bible in an arranged form. That is to say, they are not merely comments on the Bible, but they are practically the Bible itself. . . ."

WT 9/15/1910, p. 4685

A person would go into darkness after two years of reading the Bible alone; would be in the light reading the *Studies in the Scriptures* alone.

WT 9/15/1910, p. 4685

There has been no clear understanding of the Bible for centuries.

WT 9/15/1911, p. 4885

"Rather we should seek for dependent Bible study, rather than for independent Bible study."

WT 9/15/1911, p. 4885

"Any class leader who would make objection to a reference being made to *The Watch Tower* or to *Studies in the Scriptures* in connection with the discussion of any topic should properly be viewed with suspicion as a teacher."

WT 9/15/1911, p. 4885

"That it [*The Finished Mystery*] contains some mistakes is freely admitted. Even the Bible contains some."

WT 4/1/1920, p. 103

"The truth comes from the storehouse as the Lord sees necessary. . . . The Lord will open up truths as they are needed by the household of faith."

WT 6/15/1921, p. 182

64

"Sometimes a member of a class will refuse to engage in the canvasing for the books because there are some mistakes in the books. . . . As everyone knows, there are mistakes in the Bible. . . ."

WT 4/15/1928, p. 126

The Vatican belittles Bible study by claiming it is the only organization authorized and qualified to interpret the Bible.

WT 7/1/1943, p. 201

With the Bible alone many parts can be seen, but with the aid of the Watchtower publications a much more complete picture of Jehovah's purposes comes into view.

WT 3/15/1954, p. 164

"The Bible is organization-minded and it cannot be fully understood without our having the theocratic organization in mind."

WT 9/1/1954, p. 529

". . . we must recognize not only Jehovah God as our Father but his organization as our Mother."

WT 5/1/1957, p. 274

"God has not arranged for that Word to speak independently or to shine forth lifegiving truths by itself. It is through his organization God provides this light."

WT 5/1/1957, p. 274

"The world is full of Bibles. . . . Why then do the people not know which way to go? Because they do not also have the teaching or law of the mother, which is light."

WT 5/1/1957, p. 274

"He wants his earthly servants united, and so he has made understanding the Bible today dependent upon associating with his organization."

WT 11/1/1961, p. 668

"It is through the columns of *The Watchtower* that Jehovah provides direction and constant Scriptural counsel to his people. . . ."

WT 5/1/1964, p. 277

An elderly couple pray before unwrapping each issue of *The Watchtower* that God will make them worthy to see his message.

WT 9/15/1964, p. 574

"He does not impart his holy spirit and an understanding and appreciation of his Word apart from his visible organization."

WT 7/1/1965, p. 391

Heavy research is not necessary. The Watch Tower has done it for you. The most beneficial study you can do is to read *The Watchtower* or *Awake!* or a new book by the organization.

WT 6/1/1967, p. 338

". . . the Bible is an organizational book. . . . For this reason the Bible cannot be properly understood without Jehovah's visible organization in mind."

WT 10/1/1967, p. 587

"Jehovah's organization alone, in all the earth, is directed by God's holy spirit or active force."

WT 7/1/1973, p. 402

The Bible is a sealed book except to the organization.

WT 7/1/1973, p. 402

"How very much true Christians appreciate associating with the only organization on earth that understands the 'deep things of God'!"

WT 7/1/1973, p. 402

"*Zion's Watch Tower* of March 1880 had declared: '"The Times of the Gentiles" extend to 1914, and the heavenly kingdom will not have full sway till then.' Only God by his holy spirit could have revealed this to those early Bible students so far in advance."

WT 7/1/1973, p. 402

Jehovah caused the Bible to be written in such a way that you need his human channel to understand it.

WT 2/15/1981, p. 17

"We all need help to understand the Bible, and we cannot find the Scriptural guidance we need outside the 'faithful and discreet slave' organization."

WT 2/15/1981, p. 19

"... from among the ranks of Jehovah's people ... haughty ones ... say that it is sufficient to read the Bible exclusively, either alone or in small groups at home. But, strangely, through such 'Bible reading,' they have reverted right back to the apostate doctrines that commentaries by Christendom's clergy were teaching 100 years ago. ...."

WT 8/15/1981, pp. 28–29

"Unless we are in touch with this channel of communication that God is using, we will not progress along the road to life, no matter how much Bible reading we do."

WT 12/1/1981, p. 27

An individual must have *The Watchtower* to understand the Bible.

1983 YEARBOOK, p. 21

"Avoid independent thinking ... questioning the counsel that is provided by God's visible organization."

WT 1/15/1983, p. 22

"Fight against independent thinking."

WT 1/15/1983, p. 27

"... yet there are some who point out that the organization has had to make adjustments before, and so they argue: 'This shows that we have to make up our own mind on what to believe.' This is independent thinking. Why is it so dangerous? Such thinking is an evidence of pride."

WT 1/15/1983, p. 27

Read only the Bible? Christendom does this and look at the misunderstanding of the true message of God's Word!

WT 3/1/1983, p. 25

Association with JWs requires accepting the teachings of the Bible, including scriptural beliefs that are unique to Jehovah's Witnesses.

WT 4/1/1986, p. 31

Biography of C. T. Russell

Picture of C. T. Russell

WT 1/1/1912, p. 14

A biography of Russell

WT 12/1/1916, p. 5997

Memoirs of Pastor Russell

WT 12/15/1916, p. 6024

Overland Monthly's biography of Pastor Russell for sale

WT 5/15/1917, p. 146

"publish a volume setting forth the incidents of his [Russell's] life and work aside from and in addition to his personal writings"

WT 12/1/1923, p. 360

Biography of Pastor Russell

STUDIES, Vol. 1, 1924–27 editions, p. 1

Reference to the 1926 biography of Russell

DIVINE PURPOSE, p. 17

The organization "never published a biography of Pastor Russell."

DIVINE PURPOSE, p. 63

Blood, Vaccination, Transplants

"Vaccination is a direct violation of the everlasting covenant that God made with Noah after the flood."

GOLDEN AGE 2/4/1931, p. 293

Vaccinations appear to have caused a marked decrease in diseases.

A 8/22/1965, p. 20

Organ transplants are cannibalism, hence inappropriate for Christians.

WT 11/15/1967, pp. 702–4

Jehovah's Witnesses consider *all* organ transplants to be cannibalism, hence unacceptable.

A 6/8/1968, p. 21

Organ transplants are not necessarily cannibalistic.

WT 3/15/1980, p. 31

Abstaining from blood (Acts 15:29) "should be observed by all spiritual Israelites as representing the divine will."

WT 4/15/1909, p. 4374

In a great emergency a physician gave a quart of his own blood; today the woman lives and smiles.

CONSOLATION 12/25/1940, p. 19

"They know that if they violate God's law on blood and the child dies in the process, they have endangered that child's opportunity for everlasting life in God's new world."

BLOOD, MED., p. 54

"It may result in the immediate and very temporary prolongation of life, but that at the cost of eternal life for a dedicated Christian."

BLOOD, MED., p. 55

A pet should not be given a blood transfusion.

WT 2/15/1964, p. 127

"The issue of blood for Jehovah's Witnesses, therefore, involves the most fundamental principles. . . . Their relationship with their Creator and God is at stake."

JW ON BLOOD, pp. 18–19

"However, though leeches parasitically feed on blood in their natural state at present, it would not be proper for a Christian to permit leeches to draw his blood. . . . [That] would involve deliberately feeding blood to these creatures. That would conflict with the Bible's indication that blood, being sacred and representing life, should be disposed of if it is removed from a body."

WT 6/15/1982, p. 31

Channel of Communication

"Is not the Watch Tower Bible and Tract Society the one and only channel which the Lord has used in dispensing his truth continually since the beginning of the harvest period?"

WT 4/1/1919, p. 6414

The loyalty test: God gave C. T. Russell to the church as a mouthpiece for him. Those who claim to have learned the truth apart from C. T. Russell are deceivers. Satan will cause people to think Russell was not the channel.

WT 9/15/1922, p. 279

Angels hear the instructions and then pass it on to the remnant; they have been doing so since 1919.

VINDICATION, Vol. 3, p. 250

God is using *The Watchtower* for means of communication.

1939 YEARBOOK, p. 85

Instructions come to the Lord's people on the earth from the office of the Watchtower Society's president.

1943 YEARBOOK, pp. 226–27

The *Watch Tower* is set forth as "God's Word." (N. H. Knorr's testimony in court)

MOYLE 1943, p. 1474

"If we have love for Jehovah and for the organization of his people we shall not be suspicious, but shall, as the Bible says, 'believe all things,' all the things that *The Watchtower* brings out. . . ."

QUALIFIED '55, p. 156

The slave class is the sole channel of biblical truth.

WT 7/15/1960, p. 439

"It is through the columns of *The Watchtower* that Jehovah provides direction and constant Scriptural counsel to his people. . . ."

WT 5/1/1964, p. 277

"Jehovah's theocratically controlled organization under the immediate direction of Jehovah God himself"

WT 6/1/1965, p. 352

"the visible governing body made up of those servants whom Jehovah himself would appoint"

WT 6/1/1965, p. 352

". . . his sole visible channel, through whom alone spiritual instruction was to come. . . . recognize and accept this appointment of the 'faithful and discreet slave' and be submissive to it."

WT 10/1/1967, p. 590

"Since 1879 the *Watch Tower* magazine has been used by this collective group to dispense spiritual food regularly to those of this 'little flock' of true Christians."

WT 10/1/1967, p. 590

70

"Jesus foretold that . . . there would be a 'faithful and discreet slave' acting as his channel of communication"
WT 1/15/1969, p. 51

Jehovah's Witness organizational chart
WT 12/15/1971, p. 749

The organization is controlled altogether by God and by the forces he operates.
WT 8/1/1972, p. 458

"Through the columns of *The Watchtower* comes increased light on God's Word as Jehovah makes it known."
WT 8/1/1972, p. 460

"M'Clintock and Strong's Cyclopoedia, Volume II, page 386, says . . . 'As the Roman hierarchy was developed, the clergy came to . . . be recognized as the only priesthood and the essential means of communication between man and God.'"
1000 YEARS, pp. 377–78

"Yes, we should be deeply appreciative of all the fine spiritual food that the 'faithful and discreet slave' class has been providing through *The Watchtower*, now for ninety-four years."
WT 8/1/1973, p. 460

Jehovah caused the Bible to be written in such a way that you need his human channel to understand it.
WT 2/15/1981, p. 17

"Jehovah is not pleased if we receive that food as though it might contain something harmful. We should have confidence in the channel God is using."
WT 2/15/1981, p. 19

"Unless we are in touch with this channel of communication that God is using, we will not progress along the road to life, no matter how much Bible reading we do."
WT 12/1/1981, p. 27

"Avoid independent thinking . . . questioning the counsel that is provided by God's visible organization."
WT 1/15/1983, p. 22

"Fight against independent thinking."
WT 1/15/1983, p. 27

". . . yet there are some who point out that the organization has had to make adjustments before, and so they argue: 'This

71

shows that we have to make up our own mind on what to believe.' This is independent thinking. Why is it so dangerous? Such thinking is an evidence of pride."

WT 1/15/1983, p. 27

"To receive everlasting life in the earthly Paradise we must identify that organization and serve God as part of it."

WT 2/15/1983, p. 12

Christmas

It is quite immaterial the day Christmas is celebrated; we may properly join.

WT 12/15/1903, p. 3290

Don't quibble about the date; join in with the world and celebrate Christmas.

WT 12/1/1904, p. 3468

The *Studies in the Scriptures* suggested as Christmas gifts

WT 11/15/1907, p. 4094

Christmas is so important, regardless of the date.

WT 12/15/1926, p. 371

"Jesus was not born on December 25th. . . . Hence, celebrating his birthday through Christmas observance on December 25 is totally inappropriate for those guided by the Holy Scriptures."

WT 12/15/1979, p. 5

"We all need to face up to the fact that Christmas and its music are not from Jehovah, the God of truth. Then what is their source? . . . Satan the Devil."

WT 12/15/1983, p. 7

"Yes, Satan the Devil can ingeniously make Christmas music appear to be of God and the singing of it a Christian duty that honors Him and his Son. In reality, it does just the opposite."

WT 12/15/1983, p. 7

Communion

Clearly the loaf pictures not Jesus' body but his body members, the Christian congregation.

WT 3/15/1954, p. 174

"His body? Yes, his own body, his whole body, head and all that he was to give for them . . . the body with which he next associates his own blood when speaking of the cup."

WT 1/15/1956, p. 49

"There is only a remnant of such spiritual sons now living, and these are the ones who properly partake of the emblems. This, then, accounts for the vast majority of Jehovah's Witnesses being observers and not partakers."

WT 2/15/1985, p. 17

Cross

Cross and crown symbol

WT 1/1/1891, p. 1277

"'. . . he humbled himself, and became obedient unto death, even the death of the cross.' (Phil. 2:7, 8)"

CREATION, p. 161

"Crucifixion" (picture of Christ on the cross)

CREATION, p. 265

"The Cross" (picture)

CREATION, p. 336

". . . beginning with its issue of October 15, 1931, *The Watchtower* no longer bore the cross and crown symbol on its cover."

1975 YEARBOOK, p. 148

Justus Lipsius on how Jesus was impaled; picture also

INTERLINEAR '69, pp. 1155–56

Picture of the cross

RECONCILIATION, p. 168

Picture of the cross

HARP OF GOD, p. 115

"No biblical evidence even intimates that Jesus died on a cross."

A 11/8/1972, p. 28

Picture of Jesus with one nail through both hands

A 4/8/1974, p. 14

"So, the evidence indicates that Jesus did not die on the traditional cross."

A 9/22/1974, p. 28

Jesus had nails in his hands at John 20:19–29.

WT 1/15/1966, p. 63

"Jesus most likely was executed on an upright stake without any crossbeam. No man today can know with certainty even how many nails were used in Jesus' case."

WT 8/15/1987, p. 29

Disfellowshiping

See Shunning

Education

Heavy research is not necessary. The Watch Tower has done it for you. The most beneficial study you can do is to read *The Watchtower* or *Awake!* or a new book by the organization.

WT 6/1/1967, p. 338

Do not pursue higher education. There is very little time left! Make pioneer service, the full-time ministry with the possibility of Bethel or missionary service, your goal.

WT 3/15/1969, p. 171

Examination of Beliefs

If you get a tract or paper from us that is not in harmony with the Scriptures, let us know and do not circulate it.

WT 3/1/1894, p. 1629

We should prove by the Word of God whether the things found in *The Watchtower* are from man or from the Lord.

WT 5/1/1934, p. 131

If you find a lie, forsake it regardless of who teaches it; it is your duty to God.

RICHES, p. 178

If you have been in an organization that teaches things contrary to God's Word, forsake it.

RICHES, p. 179

". . . God . . . will not look with favor on persons who cling to organizations that teach falsehood. . . . a religion that had not been honest with you."

THIS LIFE, p. 46

The Watchtower "invites careful and critical examination of its contents in the light of the Scriptures."

WT 8/15/1950, p. 263

Do not criticize the organization. If Jehovah permits it, who are we to insist it should be different?

WT 5/1/1957, p. 284

It is not persecution for an informed person to expose a certain religion as being false.

WT 11/15/1963, p. 688

"The best method of proof is to put a prophecy to the test of time and circumstances."

WT 3/1/1965, p. 151

"Contrary to what some may think, it is not unkind and unloving to lay bare falsehood and corruption."

WT 3/1/1966, p. 132

Heavy research is not necessary. The Watch Tower has done it for you. The most beneficial study you can do is to read *The Watchtower* or *Awake!* or a new book by the organization.

WT 6/1/1967, p. 338

It is important to examine one's religion; there is nothing to fear from such an examination.

TRUTH, p. 13

Comparison between Jehovah's Witnesses and early Christianity

A 3/22/1968, p. 8

". . . adhering to false religion can mean your eternal destruction. . . . Are true Christians going to stand by quietly and say nothing about such gross misrepresentations? Hardly!"

WT 4/15/1970, p. 246

The Bible should be our primary textbook for study.

WT 4/15/1971, p. 230

Examine the evidence. Reasonable persons want to examine both sides of a matter. That is how one arrives at the truth.

A 10/22/1973, p. 6

When persons are being misled we should warn them; they may resent it, but that does not free us from the moral responsibility to give warning.

WT 1/15/1974, p. 35

There are various publications exposing Jehovah's Witnesses as heretics. We are not afraid of this.

WT 8/1/1978, p. 12

75

"Jehovah is not pleased if we receive that food as though it might contain something harmful. We should have confidence in the channel God is using."

WT 2/15/1981, p. 19

Regarding the Roman Catholic Church: Any organization that claims to be the way of salvation should be willing to submit to scrutiny and criticism.

A 8/22/1984, p. 28

title of article: "An Open or a Closed Mind—Which Do You Have?"

A 11/22/84, pp. 3–4

". . . the footnotes in *Watchtower* articles, some of which refer the reader to an older publication . . . locate that older publication and then . . . the pages referred to."

WT 6/15/1985, p. 12

"Some opposers claim that Jehovah's Witnesses are false prophets. These opponents say that dates have been set, but nothing has happened. Again we ask, What is the motive of these critics?"

WT 3/15/1986, p. 19

"If you are counseled or even reproved for some wrong practice or attitude, this, too, may prove to be an ideal time for the Devil to prompt you to ask yourself if you are in the right organization."

WT 3/15/1986, p. 16

Faithful and Discreet Slave

See also Organization

"Thousands of the readers of Pastor Russell's writings believe that he filled the office of 'that faithful and wise servant.' . . . His modesty and humility precluded him from openly claiming this title, but he admitted as much in private conversation."

STUDIES, Vol. 1, 1924–27 editions, p. 7

The 'faithful and wise servant' is one man.

STUDIES, Vol. 4, p. 613

". . . Charles Taze Russell was the messenger of the church of Laodicea."

STUDIES, Vol. 7, p. 3

"... the messenger of the Laodicean Church—'that wise and faithful servant' of the Lord—CHARLES TAZE RUSSELL."

STUDIES, Vol. 7, p. 5

"... Pastor Russell was dispensing as part of the 'food in due season' ..."

STUDIES, Vol. 7, p. 422

"the Lord's faithful and wise steward, Pastor Russell"

STUDIES, Vol. 7, p. 418

"Without a doubt Pastor Russell filled the office...and was therefore that wise and faithful servant, ministering to the household of faith meat in due season."

HARP OF GOD, 1921 edition, p. 239

"Blessed is that Servant (the whole body of Christ)"

WT 11/1881, p. 291

We are convinced that the *Watch Tower* is God's chosen vessel for dispensing "meat in due season."

WT 1/1890, p. 1171

"... those who believe in him ... 'Blessed is that *servant.*' ... they must be wise and faithful servants. ..."

WT 4/1/1895, p. 1797

In our issue of April 1, 1895, we applied "that servant" to *all* servants of God, but further examination points to *one* individual servant.

WT 3/1/1896, p. 47

The "faithful and wise steward" would not be a company of individuals.

WT 4/15/1904, p. 3356

The Lord has a particular messenger commissioned as his representative.

WT 6/1/1905, p. 3570

Mrs. Russell's view of who is the "faithful and wise servant"; one particular servant; "that servant"

WT 7/15/1906, p. 3811

"the truths I present as God's mouthpiece"

WT 7/15/1906, p. 3821

Pastor Russell held closely to the Scriptures. He believed that Christ had been present since 1874. He also admitted in private to being that "Faithful and Wise Servant."

WT 12/1/1916, p. 5998

"The Watch Tower unhesitatingly proclaims brother Russell as 'that faithful and wise servant.'"

WT 3/1/1917, p. 6049

The Scriptures indicate that Russell was chosen of the Lord from his birth. The two most prominent messengers were Paul and Pastor Russell. Russell is the servant of Matthew 24:45–47.

WT 11/1/1917, p. 6159

"No one in present truth for a moment doubts that brother Russell filled the office of the 'Faithful and Wise Servant.'"

WT 4/1/1920, p. 100

"The Society by overwhelming majority vote expressed its will in substance thus: Brother Russell filled the office of 'that Servant.'"

WT 4/1/1920, p. 101

Fulfilled prophecy—or physical facts—and the circumstantial evidence are conclusive proof that Russell filled the office of that faithful and wise servant.

WT 3/1/1922, p. 74

Those in the truth got there by the ministry of Russell. To repudiate his work is equivalent to a repudiation of the Lord.

WT 5/1/1922, p. 132

"The Lord indicated he would use one member of his Church as the channel. . . ."

WT 3/1/1923, p. 68

When asked who the faithful and wise servant was, Russell would reply, "Some say I am while others say the Society is"; both are true, since Russell was in fact the Society.

WT 3/1/1923, p. 68

"That Faithful and Wise Servant" does not apply to one individual and not to Brother Russell. Russell never made that claim himself.

WT 2/15/1927, p. 56

The faithful and wise servant occupies a place similar to that fulfilled by Timothy and Titus; the servant now acts under the direction and supervision of Jesus Christ.

WT 6/1/1938, p. 164

"What is the channel? . . . a 'faithful and wise servant' in the 'last days.' . . . The physical facts have come to pass in fulfillment of this prophecy, and they reveal the light-channel to be the Watchtower Society."

THEOCRATIC, pp. 249–50

Russell first taught that the faithful and wise servant was the organization; then the view was taught that Russell was the servant. This led to creature worship. After Russell died, Rutherford battled with those who still followed him.

DIVINE PURPOSE, pp. 68–69

Russell never claimed to be the faithful and wise servant.

1000 YEARS, p. 346

"Much earlier, in 1881 . . . it was understood that the 'servant' God used to dispense spiritual food was a class. With the passing of time, however, the idea adopted by many was that C. T. Russell himself was the 'faithful and wise servant.' . . . In February 1927 this erroneous thought that Russell himself was the 'faithful and wise servant' was cleared up."

1975 YEARBOOK, p. 88

". . . the 'servant' or 'slave' that Jesus foretold must be the members of *spiritual* Israel on earth—not an individual person, but a *body*."

WT 7/15/1976, p. 443

"In the early part of our 20th century prior to 1919, the Bible Students, as Jehovah's Witnesses were then known, had to be released from a form of spiritual captivity to the ideas and practices of false religion. . . . Some were exalting creatures, indulging in a personality cult that focused on Charles T. Russell. . . ."

WT 5/1/1989, p. 4

False Prophets

See also **Prophecies, Prophets**

"Will the people continue to be hoodwinked by these false prophets . . . or will they be guided by the plain Word of God . . . ?"

CREATION, pp. 188–89

"If these prophecies have not been fulfilled, and if all possibility of fulfillment is past, then these prophets are proven false."

PROPHECY, p. 22

"God's faithful people on the earth emphasized the importance of the dates 1914 and 1918 and 1925. They had much to say about these dates and what would come to pass, but all they predicted did not come to pass."

VINDICATION, Vol. 1, p. 146

"There was a measure of disappointment on the part of Jehovah's faithful ones on earth concerning the years 1914, 1918 and 1925. . . . they also learned to quit fixing dates for the future and predicting what would come to pass on a certain date. . . ."

VINDICATION, Vol. 1, pp. 338–39

"Jehovah . . . will put all false prophets to shame either by not fulfilling the false prediction of such self-assuming prophets or by having His own prophecies fulfilled in a way opposite to that predicted by the false prophets."

PARADISE REST., pp. 353–54

". . . their prophecies to date have not come to pass; and that alone is strong evidence that they are false prophets."

LIGHT, Vol. 2, p. 47

The difference between true and false prophets

WT 5/15/1930, pp. 153–57

A pastor prophesied the end; he was called a false prophet.

WT 10/15/1958, p. 613

It is not persecution for an informed person to expose a certain religion as being false.

WT 11/15/1963, p. 688

"The best method of proof is to put a prophecy to the test of time and circumstances."

WT 3/1/1965, p. 151

"True, there have been those in times past who predicted an 'end to the world,' even announcing a specific date. . . . The 'end' did not come. They were guilty of false prophesying. . . . Missing from such people were God's truths and the evidence that he was guiding and using them."

A 10/8/1968, p. 23

"Similarly, the 'false prophet' is not a person, but is a system or an organization."

WT 6/15/1974, p. 381

Christians cannot be wishy-washy, going back to the same teachings they had rejected earlier.

WT 5/15/1976, p. 298

". . . the great tribulation may not have come as soon as many of us had expected. . . . It draws closer with each day."

WT 2/1/1979, p. 24

"At times explanations given by Jehovah's visible organization have shown adjustments, seemingly to previous points of view. But this has not actually been the case. . . . 'Tacking' into the wind . . ."

WT 12/1/1981, p. 27

"Some opposers claim that Jehovah's Witnesses are false prophets. These opponents say that dates have been set, but nothing has happened. Again we ask, What is the motive of these critics?"

WT 3/15/1986, p. 19

". . . the need to revise our understanding somewhat does not make us false prophets."

WT 3/15/1986, p. 19

Flag

". . . every one in America should take pleasure in displaying the American flag."

WT 5/15/1917, p. 6086

"Since the Bethel Home was established, in one end of the Drawing Room there has been kept a small bust of Abraham Lincoln with two American flags displayed about the bust. This is deemed entirely proper. . . ."

WT 5/15/1917, p. 6086

"'. . . an idolatrous symbol.' . . . There are Christians today who feel similarly regarding national flags. They are Jehovah's Witnesses. . . . they decline to participate in flag ceremonies."

A 9/8/1971, p. 14

". . . we do not salute the flag of *any* nation. . . . It is because we view the flag salute as an act of worship."

SCHOOL, p. 90

Franz, Frederick W.

Frederick Franz, a scholar of Hebrew, Greek, Syriac, and Latin
FAITH MARCH, p. 182

F. Franz, knowledgeable in Hebrew, Greek, Latin, Spanish, Portuguese, German, and French
WALSH, pp. 7–8

F. Franz awarded a Rhodes scholarship
WALSH, p. 176

"I won't attempt to do that [translate into Hebrew]."
WALSH, pp. 102–3

"Frederick W. Franz . . . an eminent Bible scholar"
WT 8/1/1977, p. 463

The autobiography of Frederick W. Franz
WT 5/1/1987, pp. 22–30

"Gods"

". . . the same titles are applicable to the Church as his body. . . . soon follows the power which will, under him as our head, constitute the whole body of Christ the 'Mighty God' . . . the members of that company which as a whole will be the *Everlasting Father. . . .*"
WT 11/1881, p. 298

"Now we appear like men, and all die naturally like men, but in the resurrection we will rise in our true character as Gods."
WT 12/1881, p. 301

Greber, Johannes

"Very plainly the spirits in which ex-priest Greber believes helped him in his translation."
WT 2/15/1956, pp. 110–11

Johannes Greber cited for support.
WORD, p. 5

Johannes Greber cited for support.
MAKE SURE '65, p. 489

Johannes Greber cited for support for Matthew 27:52–53.
AID, p. 1134

Johannes Greber cited for support for John 1:1.

AID, p. 1669

Johannes Greber cited for support.

WT 9/15/1962, p. 554

Johannes Greber quoted about Matthew 27:52–53

WT 10/15/1975, p. 640

Johannes Greber cited for support.

WT 4/15/1976, p. 231

"Why, in recent years, has *The Watchtower* not made use of the translation by the former Catholic priest, Johannes Greber? . . . *The Watchtower* has deemed it improper to make use of a translation that has such a close rapport with spiritism."

WT 4/1/1983, p. 31

Heavenly/Earthly Hope

See also New Covenant, Salvation

"Num. 4:46–48 and Ex. 28:1 indicate but one priest to each 2,860 Levites, which would make the number of the Great Company approximate 411,840,000."

STUDIES, Vol. 7, p. 103

". . . the heavenly hope was held out, highlighted and stressed until about the year 1935. Then as 'light flashed up' to reveal clearly the identity of the 'great crowd' of Revelation 7:9, the emphasis began to be placed on the earthly hope."

WT 2/1/1982, p. 28

Jehovah's Witnesses entertained the "one hope" of Ephesians 4:4–6 until 1935; since 1935 they have published the earthly hope.

WT 12/15/1982, p. 19

Hell

The ancient Jews believed the wicked had no further existence beyond death.

HAPPINESS, p. 118

"Yes, good people go to the Bible hell. . . . Sheol and Hades refer not to a place of torment but to the common grave of all mankind."

LIVE FOREVER, p. 83

"... when a person is dead he is completely out of existence. He is not conscious of anything."

LIVE FOREVER, p. 88

Higher Powers

In 1929 the light broke forth. The higher powers of Romans 13 are Jehovah God and Jesus Christ.

TRUTH ... FREE, p. 312

"So, the 'higher powers' the apostle mentioned are Jehovah God and Christ Jesus. ..."

LET GOD BE, p. 248

"... following World War I ... There were many false doctrines and practices that had not yet been cleaned out of the organization. ... With considerable misunderstanding they had accepted earthly political governments as the 'superior authorities' that God had ordained according to Romans 13:1. ..."

DIVINE PURPOSE, p. 91

"God permitted the political authorities of this world to continue as the 'higher powers' or the 'powers that be,' which are 'ordained of God.'"

BABYLON GREAT, p. 548

Romans 13:1 refers to governments.

WT 5/15/1980, p. 4

Holy Spirit

"Nothing in this and similar texts involves the thought of a personal Holy Spirit ... conceived of as a person, one of a trinity of Gods. ..."

STUDIES, Vol. 5, p. 244

"We acknowledge that the personality of the Holy Spirit is the Father and the Son; that the Holy Spirit proceeds from both, and is manifested in all who receive the begetting of the Holy Spirit and thereby become sons of God."

STUDIES, Vol. 7, p. 57

"He does not impart his holy spirit and an understanding and appreciation of his Word apart from his visible organization."

WT 7/1/1965, p. 391

"Jehovah's organization alone, in all the earth, is directed by God's holy spirit or active force."

WT 7/1/1973, p. 402

"*Zion's Watch Tower* of March 1880 had declared: '"The Times of the Gentiles" extend to 1914, and the heavenly kingdom will not have full sway till then.' Only God by his holy spirit could have revealed this to those early Bible students so far in advance."

WT 7/1/1973, p. 402

"That same holy spirit and angelic direction still affect the preaching activities of Christian ministers."

WT 7/1/1973, p. 405

"Is the Devil a personification or a person? . . . Can an unintelligent 'force' carry on a conversation with a person? . . . only an intelligent person could. . . . 'Every quality, every action, which can indicate personality, is attributed to him in language which cannot be explained away.'" [Editor's note: Christians can paraphrase this argument to prove the Holy Spirit is a Person rather than an "active force" as the WT teaches.]

A 12/8/1973, p. 27

title of book: *Holy Spirit—The Force Behind the Coming New Order!*

HOLY SPIRIT, p. 1

". . . we cannot hope to receive holy spirit if we ignore the earthly channel Jehovah is using today. . . ."

WT 7/15/1987, pp. 18–19

Jesus Christ

See *also* Resurrection of Christ, Worship Christ

"'Let all the angels of God worship him' [that must include Michael, the chief angel, hence Michael is not the Son of God]."

WT 11/1879, p. 48

Jesus is the Alpha and the Omega, the Almighty, of Revelation 1:8.

STUDIES, Vol. 7, p. 15

Michael in Revelation 12:7 is the pope of Rome.

STUDIES, Vol. 7, p. 188

Jesus is the Alpha and the Omega of Revelation 21:6.

STUDIES, Vol. 7, p. 318

Romans 10:14 refers to Jesus.

WT 12/1/1903, p. 3282

Romans 10:14–16 refers to Jehovah.

WT 7/1/1940, p. 200

In due time God exalted Jesus to the highest position a creature could be given.

A 9/22/1959, p. 7

"There is Scriptural evidence for concluding that Michael was the name of Jesus Christ before he left heaven and after his return."

WT 5/15/1969, p. 307

Watchtower's answer for John 1:1

WT 11/15/1975, p. 702

In Romans 10:12 the identity of the "Lord" cannot be established with certainty from the context.

WT 2/1/1977, p. 95

Romans 10:13 is referring to Jesus.

WT 5/1/1978, p. 12

Revelation 22:12 is referring to Jehovah.

A 8/22/1978, p. 28

Revelation 22:7, 12, 20 is referring to Jesus.

WT 10/1/1978, p. 15

Romans 10:13 is referring to Jehovah.

WT 2/1/1980, p. 16

Does it matter what you believe about Jesus? Yes!

WT 2/1/1984, p. 3

"'Michael the great prince' is none other than Jesus Christ himself.—Daniel 12:1"

WT 12/15/1984, p. 29

"In such a way the heavenly Father of Jesus Christ will become the heavenly Grandfather of the restored human family."

WORLDWIDE, p. 169

"In answer Thomas said to him: 'My Lord and my God!'—John 20:28" (Interlinear reading, literally: "The Lord of me and the God of me!") [Editor's note: The interlinear Greek shows *ho theos.*]

INTERLINEAR '85, p. 513

"How could Jesus be 'a god' . . . ?"

WT 7/1/1986, p. 31

"The title *ho theos* [the God, or God] . . . is not applied in the N[ew] T[estament] to Jesus. . . ." [Editor's note: See John 20:28, where *ho theos* is applied to Jesus.]

WT 7/1/1986, p. 31

Lie

"Did she tell a lie? No, she did not. She was not a liar. Rather, she was using theocratic war strategy, hiding the truth by action and word for the sake of the ministry."

WT 5/1/1957, p. 285

Lying to God's enemies is not really lying but war strategy.

WT 6/1/1960, p. 352

"While malicious lying is definitely condemned in the Bible, this does not mean that a person is under obligation to divulge truthful information to people who are not entitled to it."

AID, p. 1061

"While malicious lying is definitely condemned in the Bible, this does not mean that a person is under obligation to divulge truthful information to people who are not entitled to it."

INSIGHT, p. 245

Marriage

"Would it be Scripturally proper for them to now marry and begin to rear children? No, is the answer, which is supported by the Scriptures."

FACE FACTS, p. 46

"Those Jonadabs who now contemplate marriage, it would seem, would do better if they wait a few years, until the fiery storm of Armageddon is gone. . . ."

FACE FACTS, pp. 49–50

"We can well defer our marriage until lasting peace comes to the earth."

CHILDREN, p. 366

Should they marry now? No, is the answer supported by the Scriptures.

WT 11/1/1938, p. 323

There is no reasonable or scriptural injunction to bring children into the world before Armageddon, where we are now.

WT 11/1/1938, p. 324

Forbidding to marry is wrong.

WT 4/1/1964, p. 199

Bridal veil and white dress have possible pagan origins.

WT 1/15/1969, p. 60

Wedding ring has possible pagan origins.

WT 1/15/1972, p. 63

Certain specific forms of contact are ruled improper between husband and wife in the marriage bed. Married couples must avoid these practices; otherwise, they may be disfellowshiped by the elders.

WT 12/1/1972, pp. 734–36

A great crowd of people are confident that great destruction is imminent, which has been a major factor in their decision not to have children.

A 11/8/1974, p. 11

Those who forbid marriage have departed from the faith.

WT 9/15/1979, p. 31

"Shocking as it is, even some who have been prominent in Jehovah's organization have succumbed to immoral practices, including homosexuality, wife swapping, and child molesting."

WT 1/1/1986, p. 13

"But separation is allowable if an unbelieving mate's opposition (perhaps including physical restraint) makes it genuinely impossible to pursue true worship and imperils the believer's spirituality."

WT 11/1/1988, p. 22

". . . if a baptized marriage partner acts like an apostate and tries to prevent his mate from serving Jehovah, the elders should handle matters. . . . a legal separation would not be going against Paul's counsel about taking a believer to court."

WT 11/1/1988, p. 23

Military Service

"If, therefore, we were drafted, and if the government refused to accept our conscientious scruples against warfare . . . we should request to be assigned . . . to some other non-combatant place of usefulness. . . . If not, and we ever got into battle, we might help to terrify the enemy, but need not shoot anybody."

WT 7/1/1898, p. 2332

"no command in the Scriptures against military service"

WT 8/1/1898, p. 2345

"nothing against our consciences in going into the army"

WT 4/15/1903, p. 3180

A narrow-minded Christian during wartime might object to serving with the Red Cross or buying government bonds, but a scripturally informed Christian sees it is proper to do both.

WT 6/1/1918, p. 6268

Due to conscience, Jehovah's Witnesses refuse military service.

WT 2/1/1951, p. 73

Should you defend yourself? A homeowner has the right to inflict hard blows. Jesus' apostles had at least two swords.

WT 9/8/1975, pp. 27–28

". . . Jehovah's Witnesses . . . have also declined to do noncombatant service or to accept other work assignments as a substitute for military service."

UNITED, p. 167

New Covenant

See also **Heavenly/Earthly Hope, Salvation**

". . . the '*New* Covenant' is a thing of the future."

WT 6/1880, p. 110

". . . the New Covenant is now in force, having been sealed by the blood, the death of Christ."

WT 9/1887, p. 974

". . . the work of the Christ in the inauguration of the New Covenant could not begin until the perfecting of his own body, which is the church. . . . and all of his blood has not yet been shed."

WT 4/1/1909, p. 4367

New World Translation

See also Greber, Johannes

"We offer no paraphrase of the Scriptures. . . . as literal a translation as possible . . . as nearly as possible, word for word, the exact statement of the original. We realize that sometimes the use of so small a thing as the definite or indefinite article or the omission of such may alter the correct sense of the original passage."

N.W.T., 1950, p. 9

Our salvation depends on the correct translation of John 1:1.

WORD, p. 52

One of the various ways in which the *New World Translation* honors God is by avoiding trinitarian bias.

WT 12/15/1963, p. 763

"In answer Thomas said to him: 'My Lord and my God!'—John 20:28" (Interlinear reading, literally: "The Lord of me and the God of me!") [Editor's note: The interlinear Greek shows *ho theos*.]

INTERLINEAR '85, p. 513

"The title *ho theos* [the God, or God] . . . is not applied in the N[ew] T[estament] to Jesus. . . ." [Editor's note: See John 20:28, where *ho theos* is applied to Jesus.]

WT 7/1/1986, p. 31

"But when he again brings his First-born into the inhabited earth, he says: 'And let all God's angels worship him'" (Heb. 1:6).

N.W.T., 1961, p. 1293

"But when he again brings his Firstborn into the inhabited earth, he says: "And let all God's angels do obeisance to him" (Heb. 1:6).

N.W.T., 1971, p. 1293

". . . and the Word was a god" (John 1:1).

N.W.T., 1981, p. 1151

Organization

See also Faithful and Discreet Slave

"We believe that a visible organization, and the adopting of some particular name, would tend to increase our numbers and make us more respectable in the estimation of the world. . . . But . . . We always refuse to be called by any other name than that of our Head—Christians. . . ."

WT 3/1883, p. 458

There is no organization today clothed with authority.

WT 9/1/1893, p. 1573

A visible organization is out of harmony with God's divine plan.

WT 12/1/1894, p. 1743

"Beware of 'organization.' It is wholly unnecessary."

WT 9/15/1895, p. 1866

"In 1879 Charles Taze Russell began the publication of THE WATCH TOWER, of which he was the sole editor as long as he remained on earth."

STUDIES, Vol. 7, p. 4

God used Pastor Russell to publish *Studies in the Scriptures.*

CREATION, p. 131

"Brother MacMillan later wrote: '. . . In essence we showed that the Society is wholly a religious organization; that the members accept as their principles of belief the holy Bible as expounded by Charles T. Russell. . . .'"

1975 YEARBOOK, p. 106

The editor of *The Watchtower* is Jehovah God according to court testimony by Frederick Franz.

MOYLE, p. 795

Jehovah God is the editor of *The Watchtower.* . . . But Judge Rutherford had charge of what went in or did not go in the magazine, according to testimony by Frederick Franz.

MOYLE, p. 866

The Lord gave Mr. Rutherford the power to write the articles, not the Board of Directors. The Board of Directors have nothing to do with doctrinal matters, according to testimony by Frederick Franz.

MOYLE, p. 899

Discussion of who "ministers" are.

KINGDOM MIN. 1/1976, pp. 3–5

A person would go into darkness after two years of reading the Bible alone; would be in the light reading the *Studies in the Scriptures* alone.

WT 9/15/1910, p. 4685

At least three in the editorial committee have approved as truth every article in *The Watch Tower.*

WT 12/1/1916, p. 5997

A biography of Russell

WT 12/1/1916, p. 5997

Brother Rutherford said: "The Watch Tower Bible and Tract Society is the greatest corporation in the world, because from the time of its organization until now the Lord has used it as His channel through which to make known the glad tidings. . . ."

WT 1/15/1917, p. 6033

"The Watch Tower Bible and Tract Society is the greatest corporation in the world, because from the time of its organization until now the Lord has used it as His channel through which to make known the Glad Tidings."

STUDIES, Vol. 7, p. 144

". . . we believe it is a safe rule to follow Brother Russell's interpretation, for the reason that he is the servant of the church, so constituted by the Lord for the Laodicean period; and therefore we should expect the Lord to teach us through him."

WT 2/15/1918, p. 6212

Those in the truth got there by the ministry of Russell. To repudiate his work is equivalent to a repudiation of the Lord.

WT 5/1/1922, p. 132

"This chronology is not of man but of God . . . of divine origin . . . absolutely and unqualifiedly correct."

WT 7/15/1922, p. 217

The loyalty test: God gave C. T. Russell to the church as a mouthpiece for him. Those who claim to have learned the truth apart from C. T. Russell are deceivers. Satan will cause people to think Russell was not the channel.

WT 9/15/1922, p. 279

No question or doubt that Jesus can and does direct every division of his organization, and that he uses holy angels to carry out his orders and direct the course of the remnant.

WT 9/1/1932, p. 263

If it is difficult to be in harmony with the organization's instructions, you had better check your standing before the Lord.

WT 12/1/1933, p. 364

"Jehovah's organization has a visible part on earth which represents the Lord and is under his direct supervision."

WT 5/1/1938, p. 169

The organization is God's and not man's. It is the Lord's representative on earth, and he uses it for his purposes.

WT 6/15/1938, p. 182

God uses *The Watch Tower* to communicate to his people; it does not consist of men's opinions.

WT 1/1/1942, p. 5

Jehovah uses the servant class to publish the interpretation after the supreme court by Christ Jesus reveals it.

WT 7/1/1943, p. 203

The governing body is appointed by Jehovah God. Its purpose is to issue directions and spiritual provisions to all God's people.

WT 11/1/1944, p. 330

The Watchtower "invites careful and critical examination of its contents in the light of the Scriptures."

WT 8/15/1950, p. 263

Meekly go along with the organization. Do not pit human reasoning, sentiment, and personal feelings against the organization.

WT 2/1/1952, p. 80

Who controls the organization? Jehovah!

WT 11/1/1956, p. 666

Respond to the directions of the organization as you would the voice of God.

WT 6/15/1957, p. 370

The slave class is the sole channel of biblical truth.

WT 7/15/1960, p. 439

"If one renders obedient service to someone or some organization, whether willingly or under compulsion, looking up to such as possessing a position of superior rulership and great authority, then that one can Scripturally be said to be a worshiper."

WT 9/1/1961, p. 525

Jehovah is pleased to use the slave class. The chief publication of Bible truth since 1879 is *The Watchtower.*

WT 6/1/1963, p. 338

"He does not impart his holy spirit and an understanding and appreciation of his Word apart from his visible organization."

WT 7/1/1965, p. 391

". . . the Bible is an organizational book. . . . For this reason the Bible cannot be properly understood without Jehovah's visible organization in mind."

WT 10/1/1967, p. 587

". . . his sole visible channel, through whom alone spiritual instruction was to come. . . . recognize and accept this appointment of the 'faithful and discreet slave' and be submissive to it."

WT 10/1/1967, p. 590

"Jehovah's organization . . . should influence our every decision."

WT 3/15/1969, p. 172

". . . idolatrous worshipers of a man-made organization . . ."

WT 12/1/1971, p. 723

"It is a theocratic organization, ruled from the divine Top down, and not from the rank and file up."

WT 12/15/1971, p. 754

"under angelic direction"

WT 4/1/1972, p. 200

The organization is controlled altogether by God and by the forces he operates.

WT 8/1/1972, p. 458

"So, recognition of that governing body and its place in God's theocratic arrangement of things is necessary for submission to the headship of God's Son."

WT 12/15/1972, p. 755

"How very much true Christians appreciate associating with the only organization on earth that understands the 'deep things of God'!"

WT 7/1/1973, p. 402

Failure to respond to the direction of the organization indicates a rejection of Divine rulership.

WT 2/15/1976, p. 124

"Put faith in a victorious organization!"

WT 3/1/1979, p. 1

"We all need help to understand the Bible, and we cannot find the Scriptural guidance we need outside the 'faithful and discreet slave' organization."

WT 2/15/1981, p. 19

"Indeed, this 'slave,' or spirit-anointed congregation, is the one approved channel representing God's kingdom on earth."

WT 3/1/1981, p. 24

". . . come to Jehovah's organization for salvation . . ."

WT 11/15/1981, p. 21

"What is your attitude toward directives from 'the faithful and discreet slave'? Loyalty should move you to be 'ready to obey.'"

WT 12/1/1981, p. 14

"an organization to direct the minds of God's people"

WT 3/1/1983, p. 25

"We must not lose sight of the fact that God is directing his organization."

WT 6/1/1985, p. 19

Pleiades

"Alcyone, the central one of the renowned Pleiadic stars . . . from which the Almighty governs his universe."

STUDIES, Vol. 3, p. 327

". . . the group Pleiades. And the reasonable suggestion has been made that that center may be the heaven of heavens, the highest heaven, the throne of God."

WT 5/15/1895, p. 1814

"The most reasonable suggestion we know of . . . namely, that heaven is located in or in connection with the heavenly group, *Pleiades.*"

WT 12/1/1896, p. 2075

". . . the Pleiades may represent the residence of Jehovah, the place from which he governs the universe."

WT 6/15/1915, p. 5710

"Suppose you should be here in 1925, what would you do? I said I believe I will be home in the Pleiades before then."

WT 11/1/1920, p. 334

"The constellation of the seven stars forming the Pleiades . . . that one of the stars of that group is the dwelling-place of Jehovah. . . . because the Pleiades is the place of the eternal throne of God."

RECONCILIATION, p. 14

". . . it would be unwise for us to try to fix God's throne as being at a particular spot in the universe."

WT 11/15/1953, p. 703

"God being an individual, a Person with a spirit body, has a place where he resides, and so he could not be at any other place at the same time."

WT 2/15/1981, p. 6

Politics

"They do not interfere with what others do as to joining a political party, running for office or voting in elections. But . . . Jehovah's Witnesses take no part whatsoever in political activities."

UNITED, p. 166

Prophecies

See also **False Prophets, Prophets**

1874

Christ's presence and the harvest began in 1874.

STUDIES, Vol. 2, p. 239

Time chart of church history

STUDIES, Vol. 3, p. 131

Second advent in 1874; the Lord took power in 1878.

STUDIES, Vol. 3, p. 234

"... a most reasonable inference ... that in the spring of 1878 all the holy apostles and other 'overcomers' of the Gospel age who slept in Jesus were raised spirit beings. ...."

STUDIES, Vol. 3, p. 234

"Our Lord, the appointed King, is now present, since October 1874, A.D. ... and the formal inauguration of his kingly office dates from April 1878, A.D."

STUDIES, Vol. 4, p. 621

"The Laodicean period of the Church extends from the fall of 1874 to the spring of 1918, three and one-half years of preparation, and forty years of harvest."

STUDIES, Vol. 7, p. 58

After the Second Adventist hopes were disappointed in 1874, Barbour convinced Russell that Christ actually returned invisibly in 1874.

STUDIES, Vol. 7, p. 54

"Fall 1874 A.D. Second Advent of the Lord"

STUDIES, Vol. 7, p. 60

"the beginning of the Times of Restitution, A.D. 1874"

STUDIES, Vol. 7, p. 64

Scriptures prove that the Lord's Second Advent was in 1874.

STUDIES, Vol. 7, p. 68

Eighty-eight proofs that the Lord's Second Advent occurred in the fall of 1874

STUDIES, Vol. 7, pp. 68–71

"... six thousand years of evil which ended in 1874."

STUDIES, Vol. 7, p. 301

"The Millennium began in 1874, with the Return of Christ."

STUDIES, Vol. 7, p. 386

"The second coming of the Lord therefore began in 1874. ...."

CREATION, p. 289 early editions, p. 310 later editions

"... the clergy would not understand these times and seasons, because they form a part of Satan's organization. ...."

CREATION, p. 291 early editions, p. 312 later editions

"To understand the events concerning the Lord's second presence from 1874 to 1914 requires one to be spiritually minded; and the clergy are not spiritually minded."

CREATION, p. 291 early editions, p. 312 later editions

"The Scriptural proof is that the second presence of the Lord Jesus Christ began in 1874 A.D."

PROPHECY, p. 65

". . . the Scriptural declaration that the Millennium of peace and blessing would be introduced by forty years of trouble, beginning slightly in 1874 and increasing until social chaos should prevail in 1914."

WT 10/1890, p. 1243

"The date of the close of that 'battle' is definitely marked in Scripture as October, 1914. It is already in progress, its beginning dating from October, 1874."

WT 1/15/1892, p. 1355

The end of 6000 years is 1873.

WT 7/15/1894, p. 1675

"Pastor Russell . . . believed and taught that we are living in the time of the second presence of our Lord, and that his presence dates from 1874. . . ."

WT 12/1/1916, p. 5998

"No one can properly understand the work of God at this time who does not realize that since 1874, the time of the Lord's return in power, there has been a complete change in God's operations."

WT 9/15/1922, p. 278

"The Scriptures show that the second presence [of the Lord] was due in 1874. . . . This proof shows that the Lord has been present since 1874."

WT 3/1/1923, p. 67

"Surely there is not the slightest room for doubt in the mind of a truly consecrated child of God that the Lord Jesus is present and has been since 1874."

WT 1/1/1924, p. 5

"From Adam's creation to the end of 1943 A.D. is 5,971 years. We are therefore near the end of six thousand years of human history. . . ."

TRUTH . . . FREE, p. 152

"In the year 1943 . . . published the book *The Truth Shall Make You Free.* . . . This moved forward the end of six thousand years of man's existence into the decade of the 1970's. Naturally this did away with the year 1874 C.E. as the date of the return of the Lord Jesus Christ. . . ."

1000 YEARS, pp. 209–10

1910

". . . this date, 1910, indicated by the Pyramid . . . we may well accept as correct the testimony of the Great Pyramid, that the last members of the 'body' or 'bride' of Christ will have been tested and accepted and will have passed beyond the vail before the close of A.D. 1910."

STUDIES, Vol. 3, early editions, p. 364

1914

By 1914 the Lord will have full control. Gentile governments will be overthrown; body of Christ will be glorified; Jerusalem will no longer be trodden; Israel's blindness will be turned away; there will be world-wide anarchy; and God's kingdom will take the place of man's governments.

STUDIES, Vol. 2, early editions, pp. 76–78

". . . within the coming twenty-six years all present governments will be overthown and dissolved. . . . the full establishment of the Kingdom of God, will be accomplished by the end of A.D. 1914."

STUDIES, Vol. 2, pp. 98–99

Above changed to "near the end of A.D. 1915" in later editions.

STUDIES, Vol. 2, pp. 98–99

". . . the 'battle of the great day of God Almighty' (Rev. 16:14.), which will end in A.D. 1914 with the complete overthrow of earth's present rulership . . ."

STUDIES, Vol. 2, early editions, p. 101

Above changed to "1915" in later editions.

STUDIES, Vol. 2, later editions, p. 101

"the full establishment of the Kingdom of God in the earth at A.D. 1914"

STUDIES, Vol. 3, p. 126

"And, with the end of A.D. 1914, what God calls Babylon, and what men call Christendom, will have passed away, as already shown from prophecy."

STUDIES, Vol. 3, p. 153

"That the deliverance of the saints must take place *some time before 1914* is manifest. . . . Just how long before 1914 the last living members of the body of Christ will be glorified, we are not directly informed." [Italics added.]

STUDIES, Vol. 3, 1913 edition, p. 228

"That the deliverance of the saints must take place *very soon after 1914* is manifest. . . . Just how long after 1914 the last living members of the body of Christ will be glorified, we are not directly informed." [Italics added.]

STUDIES, Vol. 3, 1923 edition, p. 228

"Then measuring . . . we find it to be 3416 inches, symbolizing 3416 years from the above date, B.C. 1542. This calculation shows A.D. 1874 as marking the beginning of the period of trouble; for 1542 years B.C. plus 1874 years A.D. equals 3416 years. Thus the Pyramid witnesses that the close of 1874 was the *chronological* beginning of the time of trouble. . . ."

STUDIES, Vol. 3, 1903 edition, p. 342

"Then measuring . . . we find it to be 3457 inches, symbolizing 3457 years from the above date, B.C. 1542. This calculation shows A.D. 1915 as marking the beginning of the period of trouble; for 1542 years B.C. plus 1915 years A.D. equals 3457 years. Thus the Pyramid witnesses that the close of 1914 was the chronological beginning of the time of trouble. . . ."

STUDIES, Vol. 3, 1923 edition, p. 342

". . . the great church-state systems of Europe, whose destruction began in 1914. . . ."

STUDIES, Vol. 7, p. 58

"The chronology as it appears in the STUDIES IN THE SCRIPTURES is accurate. The year 1914 brought the end of the Times of the Gentiles, but not the end of the Harvest work."

STUDIES, Vol. 7, p. 61

"Reexamine . . . Vol. 2, pages 246 and 247; change the 37 to 40, 70 to 73 and 1914 to 1918, and we believe it is correct and will be fulfilled 'with great power and glory.'"

STUDIES, Vol. 7, p. 62

"No doubt Satan *believed* the Millennial Kingdom was due to be set up in 1915. . . . Be that as it may, there is evidence that the establishment of the Kingdom in Palestine will probably be in 1925, ten years later than we once calculated."

STUDIES, Vol. 7, p. 128

Destruction of Christendom in 1914–1918

STUDIES, Vol. 7, p. 398

"The present great war in Europe is the beginning of the Armageddon of the Scriptures."

SERMONS, p. 676

"All of the Lord's people looked forward to 1914 with joyful expectation. When that time came and passed there was much disappointment. . . . They were ridiculed by the clergy and their allies in particular, and pointed to with scorn, because they had said so much about 1914, and what would come to pass, and their 'prophecies' had not been fulfilled."

LIGHT, Vol. 1, p. 194

". . . the Scriptural declaration that the Millennium of peace and blessing would be introduced by forty years of trouble, beginning slightly in 1874 and increasing until social chaos should prevail in 1914."

WT 10/1890, p. 1243

"The date of the close of that 'battle' is definitely marked in Scripture as October, 1914. It is already in progress, its beginning dating from October, 1874."

WT 1/15/1892, p. 1355

There is no reason for changing the figures; they are God's dates, not ours; 1914 is not the date for the beginning, but the end!

WT 7/15/1894, p. 1677

The trouble in October 1914 is clearly marked in Scriptures; the severe trouble to start no later than 1910, with severe spasms between now and then.

WT 9/15/1901, p. 2876

Chronological chart; 1914 begins millennial age.

WT 6/15/1905, p. 3576

"Armageddon may begin next spring, yet it is purely speculation to attempt to say just when."

WT 9/1/1914, p. 5527

101

"We did not say positively that this would be the year."

WT 11/1/1914, p. 5565

". . . our eyes of understanding should discern clearly the Battle of the Great Day of God Almighty now in progress. . . ."

WT 9/1/1916, p. 5951

In 1878 the process of setting up the kingdom began. The Lord raised the sleeping saints.

WT 6/1/1922, p. 174

"Jesus was obviously speaking about those who were old enough to witness *with understanding* what took place when the 'last days' began. . . . Even if we presume that youngsters 15 years of age would be perceptive enough to realize the import of what happened in 1914, it would still make the youngest of 'this generation' nearly 70 years old today. . . . Jesus said that the end of this wicked world would come *before* that generation passed away in death."

A 10/8/1968, p. 13

"Thus, when it comes to the application in our time, the 'generation' logically would not apply to babies born during World War I."

WT 10/1/1978, p. 31

"It is the generation of people who saw the catastrophic events that broke forth in connection with World War I from 1914 onward. . . . If you assume that 10 is the age at which an event creates a lasting impression . . ."

WT 10/15/1980, p. 31

"If Jesus used 'generation' in that sense and we apply it to 1914, then the babies of that generation are now 70 years old or older. . . . Some of them 'will by no means pass away until all things occur.'"

WT 5/15/1984, p. 5

1918

"Reexamine . . . Vol. 2, pages 246 and 247; change the 37 to 40, 70 to 73 and 1914 to 1918, and we believe it is correct and will be fulfilled 'with great power and glory.'"

STUDIES, Vol. 7, p. 62

"The seven days before the Deluge may represent seven years, from 1914 to 1921, in the midst of which 'week of years' the last members of the Messiah pass beyond the veil. . . . Our proposition is that the glorification of the Little Flock in the Spring of 1918 A.D. will be half way . . . between the close of the Gentile Times and the close of the Heavenly Way, A.D. 1921."

STUDIES, Vol. 7, p. 64

"It seems conclusive that the hour of Nominal Zion's travail is fixed for the Passover of 1918. . . . the fallen angels will invade the minds of many of the Nominal Church people . . . leading to their destruction at the hands of the enraged masses. . . ."

STUDIES, Vol. 7, p. 128

Complete overthrow of nominal spiritual Israel, i.e., Babylon, in 1918

STUDIES, Vol. 7, p. 129

". . . the destruction . . . of Christendom in 1914 to 1918 A.D."

STUDIES, Vol. 7, p. 398

"It is the Day of Vengeance, which began in the world war of 1914 and which will break like a furious morning storm in 1918."

STUDIES, Vol. 7, p. 404

"the Harvest period, from 1878 to 1918"

STUDIES, Vol. 7, p. 422

"THE CHURCHES TO CEASE TO BE . . . culminating *in 1918*, to remove it with a stroke or plague of erroneous doctrines and deeds Divinely permitted." [Italics added.]

STUDIES, Vol. 7, 1917 edition, p. 484

"THE CHURCHES TO CEASE TO BE . . . culminating *shortly*, to remove it with a stroke or plague of erroneous doctrines and deeds Divinely permitted." [Italics added.]

STUDIES, Vol. 7, 1926 edition, p. 484

"The Battle of Armageddon, to which this war is leading . . . will signify the complete and everlasting overthrow of the wrong, and the permanent establishment of Messiah's righteous kingdom."

WT 4/1/1915, p. 5659

". . . our eyes of understanding should discern clearly the Battle of the Great Day of God Almighty now in progress. . . ."

WT 9/1/1916, p. 5951

". . . the Great Pyramid, the measurements of which confirm the Bible teaching that 1878 marked the beginning of the harvest of the Gospel age. . . . the harvest would close forty years thereafter; to wit, in the spring of A.D. 1918. . . . we have only a few months in which to labor before the great night settles down when no man can work."

WT 10/1/1917, p. 6149

"What will the year 1918 bring forth? . . . The Christian looks for the year to bring the full consummation of the church's hopes."

WT 1/1/1918, p. 6191

"That the harvest began in 1878, there is ample and convincing proof. The end of the harvest is due in the spring of 1918."

WT 5/1/1918, p. 6243

1925

"No doubt Satan *believed* the Millennial Kingdom was due to be set up in 1915. . . . Be that as it may, there is evidence that the establishment of the Kingdom in Palestine will probably be in 1925, ten years later than we once calculated."

STUDIES, Vol. 7, p. 128

". . . we may expect 1925 to witness the return of these faithful men of Israel from the condition of death, being resurrected . . ."

MILLIONS, p. 88

"Therefore we may confidently expect that 1925 will mark the return of Abraham, Isaac, Jacob and the faithful prophets of old. . . ."

MILLIONS, pp. 89–90

". . . 1925 shall mark the resurrection of the faithful worthies of old. . . ."

MILLIONS, p. 97

After 1925 expect shortly Abel, Enoch, Noah, Abraham, Isaac, Jacob. . . .

WAY TO PARADISE, p. 224

The undertakers will decorate these new rooms for the resurrected ones.

WAY TO PARADISE, p. 228

"There will be no slip-up. . . . Abraham should enter upon the actual possession of his promised inheritance in the year 1925 A.D."

WT 10/15/1917, p. 6157

It is the message of the hour, that must go to all Christendom: "Millions now living will never die."

WT 10/15/1920, p. 310

"This chronology is not of man but of God . . . of divine origin . . . absolutely and unqualifiedly correct."

WT 7/15/1922, p. 217

"1914 ended the Gentile Times. . . . The date 1925 is even more distinctly indicated by the Scriptures. . . . by then the great crisis will be reached and probably passed."

WT 9/1/1922, p. 262

"1925 is definitely settled by the Scriptures. . . . the Christian has much more upon which to base his faith than Noah had (so far as the Scriptures reveal) upon which to base his faith in a coming deluge."

WT 4/1/1923, p. 106

"The year 1925 is a date definitely and clearly marked in the Scriptures, even more clearly than that of 1914."

WT 7/15/1924, p. 211

"The year 1925 is here. With great expectation Christians have looked forward to this year. Many have confidently expected that all members of the body of Christ will be changed to heavenly glory during the year. This may be accomplished. It may not be."

WT 1/1/1925, p. 3

"It is to be expected that Satan will try to inject into the minds of the consecrated the thought that 1925 should see an end of the work, and that therefore it would be needless for them to do more."

WT 9/1/1925, p. 262

Some anticipated the work would end in 1925. The Lord did not so state.

WT 8/1/1926, p. 232

"The year 1925 came and went. Jesus' anointed followers were still on earth as a class. The faithful men of old times—Abraham, David and others—had not been resurrected to become princes in the earth. (Ps. 45:16) So, as Anna MacDonald recalls: '1925 was a sad year for many brothers. Some of them were stumbled; their hopes were dashed. . . . Instead of its being considered a "probability," they read into it that it was a "certainty," and some prepared for their own loved ones with expectancy of their resurrection.'"

1975 YEARBOOK, p. 146

". . . Brother Rutherford . . . May 1–3, 1926 . . . 'It was stated in the "Millions" book that we might reasonably expect them to return shortly after 1925, but this was merely an expressed opinion.' A mistake had been made but, as Brother Rutherford stated, this was no reason to stop serving the Lord."

1980 YEARBOOK, p. 62

World War II

The Nazis will destroy the British.

FIFTH COLUMN, p. 15

". . . those faithful men of old may be expected back from the dead any day now. . . . In this expectation the house at San Diego, California, which house has been much publicized with malicious intent by the religious enemy, was built, in 1930, and named 'Beth-Sarim', meaning 'House of the Princes'. It is now held in trust for the occupancy of those princes on their return."

NEW WORLD, p. 104

". . . Job is due to be resurrected shortly with those faithful men and to appear on earth with them."

NEW WORLD, p. 130

The new book titled *Children* will prove useful "in the remaining months before Armageddon. . . ."

WT 9/15/1941, p. 288

The end of Nazi-Fascist hierarchy will come and will mark the end forever of demon rule.

WT 12/15/1941, p. 377

1975

The end of 6000 years is 1873.

WT 7/15/1894, p. 1675

Man's creation was 4026 B.C.E.; 6000 years from man's creation will end in 1975; the 7th period of 1000 years will begin in the fall of 1975.

LIFE EVERLAST., pp. 29–30

In order for the Lord Jesus Christ to be "Lord even of the sabbath day," his thousand-year reign would have to be the seventh in a series of thousand-year periods or millenniums.

APPROACHING, p. 26

Adam at age 130 had a son, Seth.

AID, p. 333

Eve at age 130 had a son, Seth.

AID, p. 538

"In what year, then, would the first 6,000 years of man's existence and also the first 6,000 years of God's rest day come to an end? The year 1975."

A 10/8/1966, p. 19

"Also, as reported back in 1960 . . . Dean Acheson declared that our time is 'a period of unequaled instability, unequaled violence.' And he warned: 'I know enough of what is going on to assure you that, in fifteen years from today, this world is going to be too dangerous to live in.'"

TRUTH, editions before 1975, p. 9

"Also, as reported back in 1960 . . . Dean Acheson declared that our time is 'a period of unequaled instablity, unequaled violence.' Based on what he knew was then going on in the world, it was his conclusion that soon 'this world is going to be too dangerous to live in.'"

TRUTH, editions after 1975, p. 9

". . . there are only about ninety months left before 6,000 years of man's existence on earth is completed. . . . The majority of people living today will probably be alive when Armageddon breaks out. . . ."

KINGDOM MIN. 3/1968, p. 4

"Hence, the first six thousand years since man's creation could be likened to the first six days of the week in ancient Israel. The seventh one-thousand-year period could be likened to the seventh day, the sabbath, of that week.—2 Pet. 3:8 How fitting it would be for God, following this pattern, to end man's misery after six thousand years of human rule and follow it with His glorious Kingdom rule for a thousand years!"

A 10/8/1968, p. 14

107

"Does this mean that the above evidence positively points to 1975 as the time for the complete end of this system of things? Since the Bible does not specifically state this, no man can say. . . . If the 1970's should see intervention by Jehovah God to bring an end to a corrupt world drifting toward ultimate disintegration, that should surely not surprise us."

A 10/8/1968, p. 14

heading of chronological chart: "6,000 Years of Human History Ending in 1975"

A 10/8/1968, p. 15

"Discussion of 1975 overshadowed about everything else. 'The new book compels us to realize that Armageddon is, in fact, very close indeed,' said a conventioner."

WT 10/15/1966, p. 629

". . . 1975 marks the end of 6,000 years of human experience. . . . Will it be the time when God executes the wicked? . . . It very well could be, but we will have to wait to see."

WT 5/1/1967, p. 262

". . . it is logical he would create Eve soon after Adam, perhaps just a few weeks or months later in the same year, 4026 B.C.E."

WT 5/1/1968, p. 271

title of article: "Why Are You Looking Forward to 1975?"

WT 8/15/1968, p. 494

"Are we to assume from this study that the battle of Armageddon will be all over by the autumn of 1975, and the long-looked-for thousand-year reign of Christ will begin by then? Possibly. . . . It may involve only a difference of weeks or months, not years."

WT 8/15/1968, p. 499

Do not pursue higher education. There is very little time left! Make pioneer service, the full-time ministry with the possibility of Bethel or missionary service, your goal.

WT 3/15/1969, p. 171

Since there is such a short time left, study no longer than six months with a prospective convert.

WT 5/15/1969, p. 312

"Would there be another creative 'day,' a seventh 'day,' at the close of the 'morning' of which the whole earth would be populated with a human family and be a global Paradise? 'Evening' of seventh creative 'day' begins, 4026 B.C.E."

ETERNAL PURP., p. 51

"'Morning' of seventh creative 'day' begins, 526 B.C.E. The first half or 'evening' period of God's seventh creative 'day' was now closing, 3,500 years from creation of Adam and Eve."

ETERNAL PURP., p. 131

"Reports are heard of brothers selling their homes and property and planning to finish out the rest of their days in this old system in the pioneer service. Certainly this is a fine way to spend the short time remaining before the wicked world's end."

KINGDOM MIN. 5/1974, p. 3

"It also tells us that this millennium must be preceded immediately by the most destructive war in all human history. We can now see the political rulers . . . being gathered . . . for that War of all wars. . . ."

WT 7/1/1974, p. 397

"The publications of Jehovah's Witnesses have shown that, according to Bible chronology, it appears that 6,000 years of man's existence will be completed in the mid-1970's. But these publications have never said that the world's end would come then. Nevertheless, there has been considerable individual speculation on the matter."

WT 10/15/1974, p. 635

A great crowd of people are confident that great destruction is imminent, which has been a major factor in their decision not to have children.

A 11/8/1974, p. 11

"Does this mean that Babylon the Great will go down by 1975? Will Armageddon be over, with Satan bound, by then? 'It could,' acknowledged F. W. Franz, the Watch Tower Society's vice-president . . . 'But we are not saying.'"

1975 YEARBOOK, p. 256

6000 years of human history will end in September, but there is a short time interval between Adam's creation and that of Eve.

WT 5/1/1975, p. 285

"... the Bible record shows ... a time lapse between the creation of Adam and that of his wife, Eve. ... Whether that period amounted to weeks or months or years, we do not know. So we do not know exactly when Jehovah's great 'rest day' began, nor do we know exactly when it will end. The same applies to the beginning of Christ's millennial reign."

WT 10/1/1975, p. 579

The time of Adam's creation can be determined, but the beginning of God's rest day cannot because there was a time lapse of unspecified length between Adam's creation and the creation of Eve.

WT 1/1/1976, p. 30

"But it is not advisable for us to set our sights on a certain date. ... If anyone has been disappointed through not following this line of thought, he should now concentrate on adjusting his viewpoint, seeing that it was not the word of God that failed or deceived him and brought disappointment, but that his own understanding was based on wrong premises."

WT 7/15/1976, p. 441

"Considerable expectation was aroused regarding the year 1975. ... Statements published that implied that such realization of hopes by that year was more of a probability than a mere possibility. It is to be regretted ... *the publication of the information* that contributed to the buildup of hopes centered on that date."

WT 3/15/1980, p. 17

"This Generation"

"Jesus was obviously speaking about those who were old enough to witness *with understanding* what took place when the 'last days' began. ... Even if we presume that youngsters 15 years of age would be perceptive enough to realize the import of what happened in 1914, it would still make the youngest of 'this generation' nearly 70 years old today. ... Jesus said that the end of this wicked world would come *before* that generation passed away in death."

A 10/8/1968, p. 13

"... the generation alive in 1914, some will see the major fulfillment of Christ Jesus' prophecy and the destruction. ...."

A 10/8/1973, p. 19

110

"Thus, when it comes to the application in our time, the 'generation' logically would not apply to babies born during World War I."

WT 10/1/1978, p. 31

"It is the generation of people who saw the catastrophic events that broke forth in connection with World War I from 1914 onward. . . . If you assume that 10 is the age at which an event creates a lasting impression. . . ."

WT 10/15/1980, p. 31

"If Jesus used 'generation' in that sense and we apply it to 1914, then the babies of that generation are now 70 years old or older. . . . Some of them 'will by no means pass away until all things occur.'"

WT 5/15/1984, p. 5

"Before the 1914 generation completely dies out, God's judgment must be executed."

WT 5/1/1985, p. 4

Awake! magazine discontinues statements in masthead about the generation that saw 1914.

A 1/8/1987, p. 4

Awake! magazine resumes statements in masthead about the generation that saw 1914.

A 3/8/1988, p. 4

"The Hebrews . . . reckon seventy-five years as one generation. . . ."

A 4/8/1988, p. 14

"Most of the generation of 1914 has passed away. However, there are still millions on earth who were born in that year or prior to it. . . . Jesus' words will come true, 'this generation will not pass away until all these things have happened.'"

A 4/8/1988, p. 14

"He [the apostle Paul] was also laying a foundation for a work that would be completed in our 20th century."

WT 1/1/1989, original magazine, p. 12

"He [the apostle Paul] was also laying a foundation for a work that would be completed in our day."

WT 1/1/1989, bound volume, p. 12

Prophets

See also **False Prophets, Prophecies**

"Truly there lived among us in these last days a prophet of the Lord. . . . his works remain an enduring witness to his wisdom and faithfulness!"

WT 6/1/1917, p. 6091

"John, dear, don't you think we should have *The Watchtower* and study it regularly, that we might be informed of the unfolding of Jehovah's prophecies?"

CHILDREN, p. 214

"The facts substantiate that the remnant of Christ's anointed disciples have been doing that prophesying to all the nations. . . ."

HOLY SPIRIT, p. 148

Who will be Jehovah's prophet? Who will be the modern Jeremiah? The plain facts show God has been pleased to use Jehovah's Witnesses.

WT 1/15/1959, pp. 40–41

Through God's agency he is having prophesying carried out. Jehovah is behind all of it.

WT 6/15/1964, p. 365

"God has on earth today a prophetlike organization."

WT 10/1/1964, p. 601

Was there a group that Jehovah would commission to speak as a prophet like Ezekiel?

WT 3/15/1972, p. 189

"This 'prophet' was not one man, but was a body of men and women. It was the small group of footstep followers of Jesus Christ, known at that time as International Bible Students. Today they are known as Jehovah's Christian witnesses."

WT 4/1/1972, p. 197

"Of course, it is easy to say that this group acts as a 'prophet' of God. It is another thing to prove it. The only way that this can be done is to review the record."

WT 4/1/1972, p. 197

Jehovah's Witnesses are not infallible or inspired prophets.

WT 5/15/1976, p. 297

112

"... the 'prophet' whom Jehovah has raised up has been, not an individual man as in the case of Jeremiah, but a class."

WT 10/1/1982, p. 27

"Under angelic direction . . . Jehovah's Witnesses today have 'everlasting good news to declare.'"

WT 12/15/1982, pp. 24–25

The three essentials for establishing a true prophet

AID, p. 1348

"God has on earth a people, all of whom are prophets, or witnesses for God . . . Jehovah's Witnesses."

A 6/8/1986, p. 9

Pyramid

fold-out diagram of pyramid

STUDIES, Vol. 1, facing p. 1

"The 'grand gallery' measures 1874 inches long at the top, 1878 inches long at a groove cut in its sides about midway between bottom and top and 1881 inches, at the bottom. . . . Now notice how aptly these three distinct dates (1874, 1878, 1881,) are marked by the pyramid. . . ."

WT 5/1881, p. 225

chronological diagram featuring pyramids

WT 9/1881, p. 272

chapter title: "The Testimony of God's Stone Witness and Prophet, the Great Pyramid in Egypt"

STUDIES, Vol. 3, 1903 edition, p. 313

"... the Great Pyramid . . . seems in a remarkable way to teach, in harmony with all the prophets, an outline of the plan of God, past, present and future. . . ."

STUDIES, Vol. 3, 1903 edition, p. 314

"Then measuring . . . we find it to be 3416 inches, symbolizing 3416 years. . . . This calculation shows A.D. 1874 as marking the beginning of the period of trouble. . . ."

STUDIES, Vol. 3, 1903 edition, p. 342

"Then measuring . . . we find it to be 3457 inches, symbolizing 3457 years. . . . This calculation shows A.D. 1915 as marking the beginning of the period of trouble. . . ."

STUDIES, Vol. 3, 1913 edition, p. 342

"The Watch Tower Society burial lots in Rosemont United Cemeteries, five miles due north of Pittsburgh City, contain ample grave space for all the members of the Bethel family. . . . In the exact center of the Bethel lot will be erected diagonally the Pyramid Shape Monument designed by Brother Bohnet, and accepted by Brother Russell . . . nine feet across the base, and its apex stone is exactly seven feet above the ground surface level."

CONVENTION REPORT, p. 7

"In the passages of the Great Pyramid of Gizeh the agreement of one or two measurements with present-truth chronology might be accidental, but the correspondency of dozens of measurements proves that the same God designed both pyramid and plan. . . ."

WT 6/15/1922, p. 187

"The great Pyramid of Egypt, standing as a silent and inanimate witness of the Lord, is a messenger; and its testimony speaks with great eloquence concerning the divine plan."

WT 5/15/1925, p. 148

"If the pyramid is not mentioned in the Bible, then following its teachings is being led by vain philosophy and false science and not following after Christ."

WT 11/15/1928, p. 341

"It is more reasonable to conclude that the great pyramid of Gizeh, as well as the other pyramids . . . were built . . . under the direction of Satan the Devil."

WT 11/15/1928, p. 344

"Then Satan put his knowledge into dead stone, which may be called Satan's Bible, and not God's stone witness. . . ."

WT 11/15/1928, p. 344

"Those who have devoted themselves to the pyramid . . . The mind of such was turned away from Jehovah and his Word."

WT 11/15/1928, p. 344

Race

Rev. William Draper, once black, is now white in answer to prayer.

WT 10/1/1900, p. 2706

"true that the white race exhibits some qualities of superiority over any other"

WT 7/15/1902, p. 3043

114

White people living in China eventually produce Chinese off-spring—without intermarrying—due to the influence of soil and climate.

WT 7/15/1902, p. 3043

Resurrection of Christ

". . . the man Jesus is dead, forever dead. . . ."

STUDIES, Vol. 5, p. 454

"We deny that He was raised in the flesh, and challenge any statement to that effect as being unscriptural."

STUDIES, Vol. 7, p. 57

"Therefore the bodies in which Jesus manifested himself to his disciples after his return to life were not the body in which he was nailed to the tree."

KINGDOM . . . HAND, p. 259

Jesus Christ was not made a human creature at his resurrection but was made a spirit, which accounts for his invisibility.

WT 4/1/1947, pp. 101–2

Jesus' fleshly body "was disposed of by Jehovah God, dissolved into its constituent elements or atoms."

WT 9/1/1953, p. 518

We are not to look for Christ to be visible to human eyes when he comes again.

WT 2/15/1955, p. 102

"The human body of flesh, which Jesus Christ laid down forever as a ransom sacrifice, was disposed of by God's power. . . ."

IMPOSSIBLE, p. 354

Jesus must be a spirit being. He simply materialized bodies.

A 7/22/1973, p. 4

". . . Jehovah God disposed of the sacrificed body of his Son."

WT 8/1/1975, p. 479

"Jesus was dead, he was unconscious, out of existence. Death did not mean a transition to another life for Jesus; rather, nonexistence."

A 7/22/1979, p. 27

"Having given up his flesh for the life of the world, Christ could never take it again and become a man once more."

LIVE FOREVER, p. 143

"In order to convince Thomas of who He was, He used a body with wound holes."

LIVE FOREVER, p. 145

Resurrection of Sodomites

The men of Sodom will be resurrected.

WT 7/1879, p. 8

The men of Sodom will not be resurrected.

WT 6/1/1952, p. 338

The men of Sodom will be resurrected.

WT 8/1/1965, p. 479

The men of Sodom will not be resurrected.

WT 6/1/1988, p. 31

The men of Sodom will be resurrected.

LIVE FOREVER, early editions, p. 179

The men of Sodom will not be resurrected.

LIVE FOREVER, later editions, p. 179

The men of Sodom will be resurrected.

INSIGHT, Vol. 2, p. 985

The men of Sodom will not be resurrected.

REVELATION, p. 273

"Some adjustments will be made in future printings of the *Live Forever* book. The only significant change is with regard to the Sodomites, on pages 178 and 179. This change appeared in the *Revelation* book, page 273, and in *The Watchtower* of June 1, 1988, pages 30 and 31. You may wish to note it in earlier printings that you have on hand."

KINGDOM MIN. 12/1989, p. 7

Russell, Charles Taze

See also **Faithful and Discreet Slave**

"In 1879 Charles Taze Russell began the publication of THE WATCH TOWER, of which he was the sole editor as long as he remained on earth."

STUDIES, Vol. 7, p. 4

"The special messenger to the last Age of the Church was Charles T. Russell. . . ."

STUDIES, Vol. 7, p. 53

"He has privately admitted his belief that he was chosen for his great work from before his birth."

STUDIES, Vol. 7, p. 53

". . . though Pastor Russell has passed beyond the veil, he is still managing every feature of the Harvest work."

STUDIES, Vol. 7, p. 144

"All Bible Students, followers of Pastor Russell . . ."

STUDIES, Vol. 7, p. 126

The Scriptures indicate that Russell was chosen of the Lord from his birth. The two most popular messengers were Paul and Pastor Russell. Russell is the "servant" of Matthew 24:45–47.

WT 11/1/1917, p. 6159

"Hence our dear Pastor, now in glory, is without doubt, manifesting a keen interest in the harvest work, and is permitted by the Lord to exercise some strong influence thereupon."

WT 11/1/1917, p. 6161

". . . we believe it is a safe rule to follow Brother Russell's interpretation, for the reason that he is the servant of the church, so constituted by the Lord for the Laodicean period; and therefore we should expect the Lord to teach us through him."

WT 2/15/1918, p. 6212

Those in the truth got there by the ministry of Russell. To repudiate his work is equivalent to a repudiation of the Lord.

WT 5/1/1922, p. 132

God used Russell to publish the *Studies in the Scriptures.*

CREATION, early editions, p. 131; later editions p. 121

"No one of the temple company will be so foolish as to conclude that some brother (or brethren) at one time amongst them, and who has died and gone to heaven, is now instructing the saints on earth and directing them as to their work."

JEHOVAH, p. 191

Some thought Russell was the faithful and wise servant; this led to creature worship.

1975 YEARBOOK, p. 88

117

"Brother Macmillan later wrote: '. . . we showed that the Society is wholly a religious organization; that the members accept as their principles of belief the holy Bible as expounded by Charles T. Russell. . . .'"

1975 YEARBOOK, p. 106

"In the early part of our 20th century prior to 1919, the Bible Students, as Jehovah's Witnesses were then known, had to be released from a form of spiritual captivity to the ideas and practices of false religion. . . . Some were exalting creatures, indulging in a personality cult that focused on Charles T. Russell. . . ."

WT 5/1/1989, p. 4

Rutherford, Joseph F.

"Following the election Brother Rutherford, addressing the meeting, said . . . 'The policies which Brother Russell inaugurated I will attempt to carry forward.'"

WT 1/15/1917, pp. 6033–34

Salvation

It is the message of the hour, that must go to all Christendom: "Millions now living will never die."

WT 10/15/1920, p. 310

Russell held the position of steward; we hold this as a fact and a necessity of faith.

WT 12/15/1922, p. 396

"To get one's name written in that Book of Life will depend upon one's works."

WT 4/1/1947, p. 204

A Christian must always be part of Jehovah's visible organization.

WT 1/1/1960, p. 19

"Parents who love their children and who want to see them alive in God's new world will encourage and guide them toward goals of increased service and responsibility."

WT 3/15/1962, p. 179

"Can it be stated flatly that only baptized Witnesses of Jehovah will survive Armageddon?" Yes, with a few exceptions.

WT 1/15/1971, p. 63

"Working hard for the reward of eternal life"
WT 8/15/1972, p. 491

"So, recognition of that governing body and its place in God's theocratic arrangement of things is necessary for submission to the headship of God's Son."
WT 12/15/1972, p. 755

Why some sins are not forgiven.
WT 8/1/1975, p. 459

". . . salvation can only be gained by . . . accepting Jesus Christ as the Son of God through whose sacrificial death salvation from sin and death was made possible."
A 1/8/1977, p. 27

". . . persons . . . will not be assured of *everlasting* life until they prove faithful against a final attack by Satan the Devil."
LIFE . . . PURPOSE, p. 177

"Put faith in a victorious organization!"
WT 3/1/1979, p. 1

"Jesus is the mediator only for anointed Christians. . . . The 'great crowd' . . . is not in that new covenant."
WT 4/1/1979, p. 31

"To keep in relationship with 'our Savior, God,' the 'great crowd' needs to remain united with the remnant of spiritual Israelites."
WT 11/15/1979, p. 26

Your attitude toward the anointed is the determining factor whether you go into everlasting cutting off or everlasting life.
WT 8/1/1981, p. 26

Those who desire life in the New Order must come into a right relationship with the organization.
WT 11/15/1981, pp. 16–17

". . . come to Jehovah's organization for salvation . . ."
WT 11/15/1981, p. 21

"Unless we are in touch with this channel of communication that God is using, we will not progress along the road to life, no matter how much Bible reading we do."
WT 12/1/1981, p. 27

". . . the heavenly hope was held out, highlighted and stressed until about the year 1935. Then as 'light flashed up' to reveal clearly the identity of the 'great crowd' of Revelation 7:9, the emphasis began to be placed on the earthly hope."

WT 2/1/1982, p. 28

Four requirements to reside forever on paradise earth

WT 2/15/1983, pp. 12–13

God has arranged for the 'good news of the kingdom' to be proclaimed so that each individual will have opportunity to work out his own salvation."

WT 2/1/1985, p. 5

The great crowd is tested as to the people's integrity, their continued faithfulness. The final test will result in Jehovah declaring them righteous.

WT 10/15/1985, p. 31

"He said: 'Unless anyone is born again, he cannot see the kingdom of God.' (John 3:3–5) . . . The 'other sheep' do not need any such rebirth, for their goal is life everlasting in the restored earthly Paradise as subjects of the Kingdom."

WT 2/15/1986, p. 14

"Who, then, may properly partake of . . . the bread and the wine? . . . Those of the 'other sheep' class are not in the new covenant and so do not partake."

WT 2/15/1986, p. 15

"Christendom's TV preachers lull millions into believing that they are 'saved' or 'born again.'"

WT 4/1/1988, p. 18

Only a limited number are born again. The great crowd does not need to be born again. Their life is earthly, not heavenly.

WT 4/1/1988, p. 18

Shunning

"Even treating the brother for a time as 'a heathen man and a publican' would not mean to do him injury, to castigate him, pillory him, or expose him to shame or contempt. . . . the brother may merely be treated in the kindly, courteous way in which it would be proper for us to treat any publican or Gentile. . . ."

WT 3/1/1919, p. 6397

"We would not refuse to treat one as a brother because he did not believe the Society is the Lord's channel."
WT 4/1/1920, p. 100

Should a Witness have business relationships with one who has been disfellowshiped?
WT 12/1/1952, p. 735

". . . a disfellowshiped relative who does not live in the same home, contact with him is also kept to what is absolutely necessary . . . even curtailed completely if at all possible."
WT 7/15/1963, p. 443

"We should not see how close we can get to relatives who are disfellowshiped from Jehovah's organization, but we should 'quit mixing in company' with them."
WT 7/15/1963, p. 444

"How should a faithful Christian act toward a relative outside the immediate family circle who has been disfellowshiped? . . . [contact with] one who does not live in the same household . . . would be much more rare than between persons living in the same home. Yet there might be some absolutely necessary family matters requiring communication, such as legalities over a will or property."
WT 6/1/1970, pp. 351–52

". . . none in the congregation should greet such persons when meeting them in public nor should they welcome these into their homes."
ORGANIZATION, p. 172

"There is, however, nothing to show that Jews with a balanced and Scriptural viewpoint would refuse to greet a 'man of the nations' or a tax collector. Jesus' counsel about greetings, in connection with his exhortation to imitate God in his undeserved kindness toward 'wicked people and good,' would seem to rule against such a rigid stand."
WT 8/1/1974, pp. 464–65

". . . if a disfellowshiped parent goes to visit a son or daughter or to see grandchildren . . . this is not the concern of the elders. Such a one has a natural right to visit his blood relatives and his offspring."
WT 8/1/1974, p. 471

". . . when sons or daughters render honor to a parent, though disfellowshiped, by calling to see how such a one's physical health is, or what needs he or she may have, this act in itself is not a spiritual fellowshiping."

WT 8/1/1974, p. 471

As of May 1974, more than 2000 had been disfellowshiped for not quitting the unclean practice of smoking.

WT 2/15/1976, p. 123

"Would upholding God's righteousness and his disfellowshiping arrangement mean that a Christian should not speak at all with an expelled person, not even saying 'Hello'? . . . a simple 'Hello' to someone can be the first step that develops into a conversation. . . . Why do Christians not greet or speak with disfellowshiped persons?"

WT 9/15/1981, pp. 24–26

"Christians related to such a disfellowshiped person living outside the home should strive to avoid needless association, even keeping business dealings to a minimum."

WT 9/15/1981, p. 29

"Previously, unbaptized ones who unrepentantly sinned were completely avoided. . . . The Bible does not require that Witnesses avoid speaking with him, for he is not disfellowshipped."

WT 11/15/1988, p. 19

Studies in the Scriptures

Sell as new truth, *Studies in the Scriptures.*

WT 3/15/1928, p. 126

Studies in the Scriptures is still for sale in 1929.

WT 11/1/1929, p. 322

In 1931 over 100,000 *Studies in the Scriptures* have been sold.

BULLETIN 12/1/1932, p. 1

Studies in the Scriptures is still being offered.

COST LIST 2/1/1944, pp. 1, 6

In announcements: *Studies in the Scriptures,* Vol. 4 is out of stock in U.S.A.

KINGDOM MIN. 7/1967, p. 3

The People's Pulpit Association changed its name in 1939 to Watchtower Bible and Tract Society, Inc.

QUALIFIED '55, p. 309

People's Pulpit Association published *The Finished Mystery.* Such a book and religious attitude tended to establish a religious sect centered around a man. In 1927 the remaining stock of *Studies in the Scriptures* were disposed of.

1000 YEARS, p. 347

Superior Authorities
See **Higher Powers**

Trinity
See also **Holy Spirit, Worship Christ**

"Moreover, the very words 'Father' and 'Son' imply a difference, and contradict the thoughts of the Trinity and oneness of person. . . . this doctrine of three Gods in one God . . . [is] one of the *dark mysteries* by which Satan, through the Papacy, has beclouded the Word and character of the plan of God."

STUDIES, Vol. 5, pp. 60–61

"How strange that any should attempt to misuse and pervert these our Lord's words, to make them support the unreasonable and unscriptural doctrine of a Trinity—three Gods in *one person.*"

STUDIES, Vol. 5, p. 76

"The Holy Spirit conceived of as a person, one of a trinity of Gods . . ."

STUDIES, Vol. 5, p. 244

"Three Gods in one person, or as some put it, one God in three persons."

WT 7/1882, p. 369

". . . the common thought of Trinitarians, that the Son *is* the Father."

WT 2/1/1899, p. 2434

". . . the common thought of Trinitarians, that the Son is the Father."

STUDIES, Vol. 7, p. 11

"We acknowledge that the personality of the Holy Spirit is the Father and the Son; that the Holy Spirit proceeds from both,

123

and is manifested in all who receive the begetting of the Holy Spirit and thereby become sons of God."
STUDIES, Vol. 7, p. 57

"Never was there a more deceptive doctrine advanced than that of the trinity. It could have originated only in one mind, and that the mind of Satan the Devil."
RECONCILIATION, p. 101

"Another lie made and told by Satan for the purpose of reproaching God's name and turning men away from God is that of the 'trinity.' That doctrine is taught by the religionists of 'Christendom' and is in substance this: 'That there are three gods in one. . . .'"
RICHES, p. 185

Mr. Benjamin Wilson (translator of the *Emphatic Diaglott*) was a Christadelphian and did not believe in the Trinity.
A 11/8/1944, p. 26

"The doctrine, in brief, is that there are three gods in one. . . ."
LET GOD BE, p. 100

The trinity is a basic false doctrine.
WT 4/1/1970, p. 210

"Is the Devil a personification or a person? . . . Can an unintelligent 'force' carry on a conversation with a person? . . . only an intelligent person could. . . . 'Every quality, every action, which can indicate personality, is attributed to him in language which cannot be explained away.'" [Editor's note: Christians can paraphrase this argument to prove the Holy Spirit is a Person rather than an "active force" as the WT teaches.]
A 12/8/1973, p. 27

title of article: "Does Christianity Require Belief in a Trinity?"
WT 2/1/1974, p. 75

"Thus the Father alone is THE God, the Supreme One, to whom all owe worship and to whom all, including the Son, are rightly subject."
WT 3/15/1975, p. 174

Christendom borrows from Plato ideas about Christ and the Trinity.
A 8/22/1976, pp. 23–26

124

The Trinity is a doctrine of Platonic origin.

WT 10/15/1978, p. 32

"God being an individual, a Person with a spirit body, has a place where he resides, and so he could not be at any other place at the same time."

WT 2/15/1981, p. 6

title of article: "The Trinity—Should You Believe It?"

WT 2/1/1984, p. 4

Encyclopedia quotes about the Trinity

WT 8/1/1984, pp. 21–22

Truth

See also Lie

"A *truth* presented by Satan himself is just *as true* as a *truth* stated by God. . . . Accept truth wherever you find it, no matter what it contradicts."

WT 7/1879, pp. 8–9

Lying to God's enemies is not really lying but war strategy.

WT 6/1/1960, p. 352

"Lying generally involves saying something false to a person who is entitled to know the truth and doing so with the intent to deceive or to injure him or another person."

AID, p. 1060

Unity

"Unity is to be along the lines of 'the faith once delivered unto the saints' in its purity and simplicity, and with full liberty to each member to take different views of minor points, and with no instruction whatever in respect to human speculations, theories, etc."

STUDIES, Vol. 6, p. 240

The Catholic Church "became powerful and used drastic methods of persecution in dealing with all not fully in accord with itself. That, however, was a unity of force, of compulsion—an outward unity, and not a unity of the heart. Those whom the Son makes free can never participate heartily in such unions, in which personal liberty is utterly destroyed."

STUDIES, Vol. 6, p. 241

"The endeavor to compel all men to think alike on all subjects, culminated in the great apostasy and the development of the great Papal system. . . ."

WT 9/1/1893, p. 1572

All JWs, though international, are of "one heart and soul," and the same line of thought.

WT 8/1/1960, p. 474

"Put faith in a victorious organization!"

WT 3/1/1979, p. 1

". . . from among the ranks of Jehovah's people . . . haughty ones . . . say that it is sufficient to read the Bible exclusively, either alone or in small groups at home. But, strangely, through such 'Bible reading,' they have reverted right back to the apostate doctrines that commentaries by Christendom's clergy were teaching 100 years ago. . . ."

WT 8/15/1981, pp. 28–29

"Avoid independent thinking . . . questioning the counsel that is provided by God's visible organization."

WT 1/15/1983, p. 22

"Fight against independent thinking."

WT 1/15/1983, p. 27

". . . yet there are some who point out that the organization has had to make adjustments before, and so they argue: 'This shows that we have to make up our own mind on what to believe.' This is independent thinking. Why is it so dangerous? Such thinking is an evidence of pride."

WT 1/15/1983, p. 27

Worship Christ

See also Jesus Christ, Trinity

"'Let all the angels of God worship him' [that must include Michael, the chief angel, hence Michael is not the Son of God]."

WT 11/1879, p. 48

"to worship Christ in any form cannot be wrong"

WT 3/1880, p. 83

"And although we are nowhere instructed to make petitions to him, it evidently could not be improper to do so; for such a course is nowhere prohibited, and the disciples worshiped him."

WT 5/15/1892, p. 1410

"Yes, we believe our Lord Jesus while on earth was really worshipped, and properly so. While he was not *the* God, Jehovah, he was *a* God."

WT 7/15/1898, p. 2337

All creatures in heaven and earth shall worship Jesus as he worships the Father.

WT 8/15/1941, p. 252

You must worship and bow down to Jehovah's chief one, namely Jesus Christ.

WT 10/15/1945, p. 313

title of subsection: "Christ to Be Worshiped"

MAKE SURE '53, p. 85

No distinct worship is to be rendered to Jesus Christ, now glorified in heaven.

WT 1/1/1954, p. 31

Stephen's prayer to Jesus at Acts 7:59

WT 2/1/1959, p. 96

Do not erroneously conclude that Christians are to worship Christ. That is not what the Bible taught.

WT 7/15/1959, p. 421

". . . it is unscriptural for worshipers of the living and true God to render worship to the Son of God, Jesus Christ."

WT 11/1/1964, p. 671

"But when he again brings his First-born into the inhabited earth, he says: 'And let all God's angels worship him.'" (Heb. 1:6)

N.W.T., 1961 edition, p. 1293

"But when he again brings his Firstborn into the inhabited earth, he says: 'And let all God's angels do obeisance to him.'" (Heb. 1:6)

N.W.T., 1971 edition, p. 1293

"In Hebrews 1:6 the Greek word *proskynéo* may mean: 1. Rendering respectful obeisance, as 'bowing down,' to Jesus as the one whom Jehovah God has honored and glorified 2. Worshiping Jehovah God through or by means of his chief representative, his Son Jesus."

WT 2/15/1983, p. 18

Appendix 1

"Watch Tower" or "Watchtower"?

"Watch Tower" or "Watchtower"—which is it? The answer is *both*. Jehovah's Witnesses are governed by a collection of legal corporations, some of which feature the name "Watch Tower" as two words and some of which spell it as one word. Moreover, the sect's principal magazine has used both spellings over the years.

In 1879 Charles Taze Russell began publishing *Zion's Watch Tower and Herald of Christ's Presence*. In 1909 he changed its name to *The Watch Tower and Herald of Christ's Presence*. Russell's successors changed the magazine's title to: in 1931, *The Watchtower and Herald of Christ's Presence;* on January 1, 1939, *The Watchtower and Herald of Christ's Kingdom;* on March 1, 1939, *The Watchtower Announcing Jehovah's Kingdom,* the title as of this writing.

In 1884 Russell incorporated the Zion's Watch Tower Tract Society, which has since been renamed and continues to function today as the Watch Tower Bible and Tract Society of Pennsylvania, the "parent" corporation of Jehovah's Witnesses.

In 1909 Russell set up operations in Brooklyn, New York, and formed the People's Pulpit Association as his legal arm there. This corporation was renamed Watchtower Bible and Tract Society, Inc. in 1939, and then in 1956 Watchtower Bible and Tract Society of New York, Inc., its present name.

A British corporation was also established in 1914 under the name International Bible Students Association. Since then, corporate bodies have also been established in other

129

lands. The primary purpose for the multiple corporations has been to meet the requirements for owning real estate under the various legal jurisdictions where the sect operates.

Although Jehovah's Witnesses worldwide are governed from offices in Brooklyn, New York, the Watch Tower Bible and Tract Society of Pennsylvania remains as the official parent corporation with ultimate financial and decision-making responsibility. There is no conflict, however, because the same leaders sit as officers and board members of the different corporations.

Appendix 2

Authorship of Watch Tower Publications

The Society's founder and first president, Charles Taze Russell, authored the first six volumes of *Studies in the Scriptures,* as well as most of the early *Watch Tower* magazine articles. But the magazines featured bylines of other staff writers and outside contributors as well. The seventh volume of *Studies in the Scriptures,* although labeled the "posthumous work of Pastor Russell," was actually written by C. J. Woodworth and G. H. Fisher.

Russell was succeeded by Joseph F. Rutherford, whose name appears as author of the other books printed during his presidency. When Rutherford was succeeded by Nathan H. Knorr in 1942, the practice was adopted of publishing everything in the name of the organization rather than an individual. Ostensibly this was to give all the glory to God and to prevent individuals from developing the pride of authorship. However, it has also been noted that Knorr was not much of a writer or theologian—administration was his forte—so lower-ranking officials became responsible for producing the publications. Defectors from Brooklyn headquarters have identified some of these authors in recent years, but for Jehovah's Witnesses (who are not allowed to read exposés written by ex-members) their identities remain closely kept secrets.

Appendix 3
Documentation

Many Watch Tower publications dated 1930 or later are still available in the "Theocratic Library" at local Jehovah's Witness Kingdom Halls, whereas the older books and magazines have generally been removed due to outdated content. But the older books can still be found in the personal libraries of many long-time JWs and former Witnesses, and in the collections of countercult Christian ministries. Some of them can be readily obtained through bookstores specializing in used or rare volumes. Photocopies of specific pages can be obtained at public libraries in many localities through inter-library services.

The following books currently in print contain photographic documentation of many of the Watch Tower quotes referenced in this *Index*. In most cases the entire page in question is reproduced.

Cetnar, William I. *Questions for Jehovah's Witnesses.* Kunkletown, PA: self-published, 1983.

Franz, Raymond V. *Crisis of Conscience.* Atlanta: Commentary Press, 1983.

Magnani, Duane, and Arthur Barrett. *The Watchtower Files: Dialogue with a Jehovah's Witness.* Minneapolis: Bethany House Publishers, 1985.

Reed, David A. *How to Rescue Your Loved One from the Watchtower.* Grand Rapids: Baker Book House, 1989.

Watters, Randall. *Thus Saith . . . The Governing Body of Jehovah's Witnesses.* Manhattan Beach, CA: Bethel Ministries, 1982.

Appendix 4

Bibliography
and
Key to Abbreviations

A	*Awake!* magazine	
AID	*Aid to Bible Understanding*	1969
APPROACHING	*The Approaching Peace of a Thousand Years*	1969
BABYLON GREAT	*"Babylon the Great Has Fallen!" God's Kingdom Rules*	1963
BLOOD, MED.	*Blood, Medicine and the Law of God*	1961
BULLETIN	*The Bulletin* monthly[1]	
CHILDREN	*Children*	1941
CONSOLATION	*Consolation* magazine[2]	
CONVENTION REPORT	Souvenir Report of the Bible Students Convention	1919
COST LIST	an internal publication listing literature available to JW congregations	
CREATION	*Creation*	1927
DEFENDING	*Defending and Legally Establishing the Good News*	1950
DIVINE PURPOSE	*Jehovah's Witnesses in the Divine Purpose*	1959
ETERNAL PURP.	*God's "Eternal Purpose" Now Triumphing for Man's Good*	1974
FACE FACTS	*Face the Facts*	1938

	Matthew A. Howlett, Watch Tower Bible and Tract Society (a Pennsylvania corporation), and Watchtower Bible and Tract Society Inc., (a New York membership corporation)—New York Supreme Court, Appelate Division, Kings County Clerk's Index No. 15845—Year 1940. This is a court transcript, not a Watch Tower publication, but it contains sworn testimony of Watch Tower officials.	
NEW WORLD	*The New World*	1942
N.W.T., 1950	*New World Translation of the Christian Greek Scriptures*	1950
N.W.T., 1961	*New World Translation of the Holy Scriptures*, 1961 revision	1961
N.W.T., 1971	*New World Translation of the Holy Scriptures*, 1971 revision	1971
N.W.T., 1981	*New World Translation of the Holy Scriptures*, 1981 revision	1981
1000 YEARS	*God's Kingdom of a Thousand Years Has Approached*	1973
ORGANIZA-TION	*Organization for Kingdom-Preaching and Disciple-Making*	1972
PARADISE REST.	*Paradise Restored to Mankind—by Theocracy*	1972
PROPHECY	*Prophecy*	1929
QUALIFIED '55	*Qualified to Be Ministers*, 1955 edition	1955
RECONCILIA-TION	*Reconciliation*	1928
REVELATION	*Revelation—Its Grand Climax at Hand*	1988
RICHES	*Riches*	1936
SALVATION	*Salvation*	1939
SCHOOL	*School and Jehovah's Witnesses*	1983
SERMONS	*Pastor Russell's Sermons*	1917
STUDIES, Vol. 1	*Studies in the Scriptures*[3], Vol. 1, *The Divine Plan of the Ages*	1886
STUDIES, Vol. 2	*Studies in the Scriptures*[3], Vol. 2, *The Time Is At Hand*	1888
STUDIES, Vol. 3	*Studies in the Scriptures*[3], Vol. 3, *Thy Kingdom Come*	1891
STUDIES, Vol. 4	*Studies in the Scriptures*[3], Vol. 4, *The Battle of Armageddon*	1897
STUDIES, Vol. 5	*Studies in the Scriptures*[3], Vol. 5, *At-One-Ment Between God & Man*	1899
STUDIES, Vol. 6	*Studies in the Scriptures*[3], Vol. 6, *The New Creation*	1904

STUDIES, Vol. 7	Studies in the Scriptures, Vol. 7, The Finished Mystery	1917
THEOCRATIC	Theocratic Aid to Kingdom Publishers	1945
THIS LIFE	Is This Life All There Is?	1974
TRUTH	The Truth That Leads to Eternal Life	1968
TRUTH ... FREE	"The Truth Shall Make You Free"	1943
UNITED	United in Worship of the Only True God	1983
VINDICATION, Vol. 1	Vindication, Volume 1	1931
VINDICATION, Vol. 2	Vindication, Volume 2	1932
VINDICATION, Vol. 3	Vindication, Volume 3	1932
WALSH	The Douglas Walsh Trial, court transcript. This is not a Watch Tower publication, but contains sworn testimony of Watch Tower officials.	1954
WAY TO PARADISE	The Way to Paradise	1924
WORLDWIDE	Worldwide Security Under the "Prince of Peace"	1986
WORD	"The Word"—Who Is He? According to John	1962
WT	The Watchtower magazine[4]	
1939 YEARBOOK	1939 Yearbook of Jehovah's Witnesses	1938
1943 YEARBOOK	1943 Yearbook of Jehovah's Witnesses	1942
1975 YEARBOOK	1975 Yearbook of Jehovah's Witnesses	1974
1980 YEARBOOK	1980 Yearbook of Jehovah's Witnesses	1979
1983 YEARBOOK	1983 Yearbook of Jehovah's Witnesses	1982

---

[1] The Bulletin was an in-house monthly instruction paper for Watchtower followers. Its name was changed to Director in October 1935; to Informant in July 1936; to Kingdom Ministry in September 1957; to Kingdom Service in January 1976; and to Our Kingdom Ministry in January 1982.

[2] The Golden Age was renamed Consolation in 1937 and Awake! in 1946.

[3] Originally called the Millennial Dawn series, the six volumes were later called Studies in the Scriptures.

[4] Zion's Watch Tower and Herald of Christ's Presence was renamed The Watch Tower and Herald of Christ's Presence in 1909, The Watchtower and Herald of Christ's Presence in 1931, The Watchtower and Herald of Christ's Kingdom in January 1939, and The Watchtower Announcing Jehovah's Kingdom in March 1939.